ENVIRONMENTAL AND ECOLOGICAL ISSUES IN INDIA

ENVIRONMENTAL AND ECOLOGICAL ISSUES IN INDIA

M. PERUMAL
R. VEERASEKARAN
M. SURESH
M. ASAITHAMBI

ABHIJEET PUBLICATIONS
DELHI 110094

ABHIJEET PUBLICATIONS
2/46 Tukhmeerpur Extension
Delhi 110094
Phones: 011-22960492, 65698474
e-mail: abhijeetpublication@gmail.com
abhijeet singh1@indiatimes.com

ENVIRONMENTAL AND ECOLOGICAL ISSUES IN INDIA

First Published 2008

ISBN 978-81-89886-29-5

Price: Rs. 450/- (INR)

PRINTED IN INDIA

Published by J.K. Singh fo Abhijeet Publications, Delhi 110094, Lasertypeset by Gaurav Graphics, Delhi and Printed as Himanshu Printers, Delhi.

Mariyappa Pillai (Curriculum Teacher)
and Angammal

M. Perumal

Preface

Establishment of a socialistic pattern of society pattern of society is enshrined in our constitution. Economic growth with equity has been the approach of development in our planning process. Basic need provision and poverty alleviation have been given priority in view of existence of acute poverty in our country. In the past 50 years, development has been achieved but at heavy cost to human health and quality of environment—our natural sustaining force. Similar trends are available at Global level too.

Realizing the importance of this issue, World Community organized Stockholm conference in 1974 and followed it by Rio-summit in 1992. Concurrently, World Commission on Environment and Development was also established in 1974. All these events highlighted the need of sustainable development and protection of environment. Agenda 21 of Rio-conference defined sustainable development is the objective an sustainability is the adjective. Therefore, both have to be combined for real benefit to the society.

Water resource development is one of the many important developments, is one many important development activities taken up by governments in many countries, being predominantly agricultural economy. Water resource development through large dams has been a popular for quite some time. But these have also attracted many criticisms and debate internationally. They have contributed in economic development, electricity generation, flood control and irrigation. Yet, their adverse environmental, social and economic impacts are increasingly noted.

AUTHORS

Acknowledgements

To thank profusely Scholars and Authorities is a pleasure indeed.

I am greatly indebted to Theiva Thirumakan Urumu Seshalam Chettiyar founder Urumu Dhanalakshmi College, Sri. G.R Kalki Varatharajulu President, Seva Ratna Mothi. S. Rajagobal, Secretary, Sri. Mothi. S. Pattabiraman Treasurer and former Principals Navukkuarasar, Dr. S. Sathyaseelan, member of Urumu Dhanalakshmi College Council and Dr. S. Surya Moorthy for their constant encouragement.

I owe my sincere thanks to respected Principal Senthamizh Thilagam Dr. K. Sekar for his timely help.

My special thanks to Dr. R. Swaminatha Ratnam, Professor and Head of the Department of Economics, for helping me in all matters of the book formation.

I take this opportunity to express my heartfelt thanks to my beloved colleagues Dr. T. Semban, Dr. S.M. Suiya Kumar, Dr. T. Meera, Dr. K. Kamar Kahan, Dr. A. Jabamalai Raja, Prof. K. Kaliyamoorthy and Prof. P. Soundarajan for their constructive criticism in this work.

My affectionate and heart felt thanks to beloved Brother-in-laws K. Karunanakaran B.Sc., and K. Arulanadam for their financial support in this work.

I owe my affectionate thanks to Dr. N. Subramani Head, Department of Bank management and my beloved friend Dr. M.Murugesan for their excellent help. My sincere thanks to Dr. R. Rajkumar Prof. and Head Department of Economics, University of Madras I.D.E. for his enthusiastic help.

My special thanks to Dr. R. Thiyagarajan, Professor and Head of the Department of Physics and Dr. S. Sekar, Professor and Head of the Department of Commerce and Dr. D. Kumar, Reader in Economics, Jamal Mohamed College, Trichy for their constructive criticism in bringing out this book in an efficient manner.

I owe my heart felt thanks to Er. Balan BE., RR Construction Trichy, Mr. Manivannan B.Com., MA., MBA., Professional Software Engineer Coliseum Technology, Chennai. Dr. A. Karunanidhi HOD of Tamil Urumu Dhanalakshmi College, and Dr. Chinkkamalliah IIM for their constant encouragement. I will be failing in my duty if I do not express my affectionate thanks to slum dewellers

I feel happy to thank my Father-in-law Mr. Kandasamy Pillai Theater Owner and my wife Mrs. Kalaivani, B.A., without their constant pressure and co-operation, I could not have visited centers of learning for data collection.

I will be failing in my duty if I could express my profound thanks to my daughter Er. Manju Shalini, B.E., and my twin sons Mr. Manoj and Mr. Vinoj for their timely help in bringing this took in time.

My profound thank to my beloved elder sisters Srimathies Meenabambikai, Kamatchi, Logambal and Koushalya whose put me in the right and pious path in my life.

I owe my sincere thanks to my mentor Shree G. Natarajan B.A., Proprietor, Rasi Hardware's Nammakkal, Salem and my cousin brother Mr. M. Sundaraj Plantain Merchant for their moral and financial support to undertake this research.

I have a long list of well wishers who inspired me in preparing this book. To save space I omit their names. I however take solace from John Keat's words "Heard melodies are Sweet those un heard are Sweeter".

My profound thanks are to Miss. K. Sangeetha Lakshmi M.Com (FM)., for her excellent help in this task.

I am thankful to Sri J.K. Singh, Abhijeet Publications Delhi, Mr. A. Sagayaraj, and Mrs. Mary Sona Santhan B.Sc., for their interest and cooperation in publishing this book.

I do not claim that I could cover all the aspects of the Environmental and Ecological Issues in India. Within the limited space, but I firmly believe that this book will be very useful to all concerned.

M. PERUMAL

Contents

Preface *vii*

Acknowledgements *ix*

1. Introduction 1

2. Environment and Pollution 8

3. Environmental Protection Acts 36

4. India and Its Ecosystem 62

5. Sustainable Development of Water Resource 122

6. Statistical Evidence of Environmental Perception 147

Bibliography 189

Index 199

1

Introduction

Earth is the only planet so far known, to have an environment that can sustain life. Environment has been defined as the sum total of all conditions and influences that affect the development and life of organisms.

There was a time when we could take pride in the scientific achievements which have as the capability to control, transform and exploit the natural environment to our will. But, today we are face to face a severe environmental crisis essentially due to indiscriminate use of this capability. Further more, the problem is not related to any particular country or region; rather it is global.

The concept of "environment" is often considered in a limited way to represent only the physical world around us. It is necessary to extend this definition to include not merely the biophysical natural environment, but also the man-made physical environment as well as the political, economic, cultural, technological, social and aesthetic environment.

Environment conditions are not merely given but also created by the human beings themselves. It is therefore, essential to conceive of environment in a holistic manner as the sum total of all conditions and influences—physical, biological, social and cultural—which affects the development and life of organisms on this planet. The environment is to be viewed as a dynamic system in which the sub-systems are in constant interaction with each other and undergoing continuous change.

Environment pollution appears to be a necessary evil of all development. It is particularly attributed to urban industrial development. Man inhabits two worlds. One is the natural world of planets and animals, soils and waters, of which he is a part. The other is the world of social institutions and artefacts, his tools and science and of his dreams to fashion an environment obedient to human purpose and direction. It is difficult to imagine that man as a species could survive after impoverishing and polluting nature.

Pollution may be defined as all those activities conscious or unconscious of human beings, which detract in anyway, directly or indirectly, from the enjoyment of environment and the ability to derive full benefit, there from. Pollution occurs when as a result of human activities, enough of such substance is generated in environment as to create harmful effects. A substance is called a pollutant if it adversely alters the environment by changing the growth rate of species, interferes with the health, comfort, amenities or properties values of the people.

Pollutants may be solid, liquid or gaseous. Pollutants may be classified into two groups, that is, visible and invisible. Visible pollutants include chimney smoke, wastewater from domestic or industrial sources, and garbage, often disposed off improperly at various bacterial species and viruses, which are a hazard to human health. The general cause of environmental pollution in an urban ecosystem can be classified under five main heads:

The pollution of the air,

The pollution of water,

Solid waste pollution,

Noise pollution, and

Social pollution

In addition to those, poverty and underdevelopment are also pollutants in every Indian village and city. Besides adding their quota to pollution, they adversely affect the quality of human life.

Man began utilizing environmental resources to meet the need of the fast multiplying number as well as to provide for a better living. However in this process, man has trespassed too far to the extent of causing serious ecological and environmental problems.

Air pollution is one of the commonest forms of environmental deterioration in the cities of both the developed and the developing countries. Air pollution refers to those conditions in which general atmosphere contains substances in concentrations, which are harmful to man or his environment or which interferes directly or indirectly with man's comfort, safety or health.

As a result of increased industrialization the percentage of carbon monoxide and sulphur dioxide is increasing in the atmosphere. The unabated use of insecticides and pesticides and the industrial and nuclear fallout's fly ash and particulates are increasing pollution in alarming proportions in the atmosphere. Moving and point sources pollute air, Automobiles, Ships aircraft and rockets represent mobbing sources. Industries and thermal power plants are examples of point sources. Air pollution is most visible. It affects living organisms significantly. Apart from creating problems of poor visibility, dust pollution causes respiratory diseases include pneumoconiosis, caused by inhalation of dust, including silicosis and asbestosis, eyes ailments include cataract, conjunctivitis, corneal ulcers, and squint trachomia.

Untreated industrial waste and city garbage disposed off in the oceans is toxic to marine life. Water pollution in most of the rivers, lakes and reservoirs of the county has increased and their water is not considered safe for human consumption without proper treatment. Water pollution is the most important. Cause of public health problem both in urban and rural areas. Waterborne diseases, such as cholera, Typhoid, diarrhoea, dysentery malarial and intestinal worms claim a heavy toll of life.

Land pollution in urban centres is due to large amounts of solid wastes which are not properly disposed. Solid waste may be defined as unwanted or discarded material in solid form resulting from resulting form normal practice of the communities. Solid waste or city refuse is produced as a result of human activity. The quantity and quality of waste varies with standard of living type of community and urban management. In spite of instructions to the contrary the people find the streets and roads ideal places for throwing out rubbish. There are mounds of household garbage on the streets, just outside the houses. Therefore, streets, roads and various localities remain strewn with waste materials of all types. Stray cattle are other sources for polluting the roads and streets. Children are seen defecating on the streets and lanes.

The main sources of noise pollution are automobiles and loudspeakers. At places industries and trains also contribute their quota. Everyday public meeting and processions by numerous political and social groups make and create too and much noise. The barking of stray dogs, clatter of utensils and habit of talking loudly adds to environmental noise. Marriage procession on an average produces about 75 to 80 decibels of noise, public meeting about 85 to 90 decibels motor cycles and heavy trucks about 90 loud speakers about 110 and commercial aircraft about 120 to 140 decibels.

Noises of modern society have an adverse impact on human health and physical system. The efficiency of a person is reduced and damaged affection the sense organs and nervous system. Noise can be damaging the human ear. Many emotional and behavioural problems occur apart from rise in blood pressure, mental abnormalities in foetus, headaches etc.

Social pollution refers to those aspects of urban problems such as problems of residence including housing congestion on the hand and on other hand are the problems of population such as child labour, beggars exploitation and corruption inadequate and bad housing, insufficient community facilities and services, social exploitation and maladjustment. Haphazard growth of cities without increasing concomitant social costs causes lack of parks in schools, water supply and other facilities for a healthy social life, thus contributing to social pollution of urban life.

One environmental aspect of transportations facilities largely ignored is that of light pollution. In many areas light pollution has become an important aspect of both planning and design. Neighbourhoods are becoming more sensitive to the stray light that is being directed towards their property and windows.

Astronomers and observations are becoming more concerned with the increase in the sky glow around urban areas. It has been estimated by researchers that up to 50% of all light pollution may be the result or roadway lighting. This firmly puts light pollution in the hands of traffic engineers and it will become their responsibility to find adequate and economic solutions.

Thus man has caused many a serous environmental problems of air pollution water pollution solid waste pollution noise pollution and social pollution. After having gone too far in polluting nature man has of late come to realize that the time has come take remedial measures.

Environmental perception, education and awareness play a most significant role in the management of environment. To the extent to which the citizens understand and appreciate the value of environment for aesthetics, health and happiness they will be found responsive and cooperate safeguarding, the environment individually and cooperatively. These differences can be observed in different cultures, levels of awareness and the state of environment in different regions and countries.

Environmental perception has been defined as the process of taking cognizance of a sensible or a quasi-sensible object, or the process of becoming aware of something. Thus environmental perception is the process of taking cognizance of the environment. This process is not a simple as it appears to be as it is based on custom culture faith, objectives and experience and differences form person to person. The environmental crisis extends to both the developing and the developed countries of the world. To natural hazards is added the quota of technological hazards exposing man and nature to ever increasing risk zones. Solutions to environmental problems and to environmental management need a priori clear perception about them. Without proper understanding of the base of perception and behaviour, environment planning and management cannot succeed. There need to know how the people see the environmental problems of the area in which they live and how that perception affects action, at the people and the organizational level. A clearer perception stimulus awareness and encourages peoples participation in creating better environmental condition. But perception may vary according to culture and mythology and religion and stage of education and development.

Individuals and groups of people relate to the environment through their perception or cognition of them. Slums are created mainly because of poverty, social backwardness and unemployment of the people living in the country side who subsequently move to urban areas without any other option. Due to drought or other unfavourable conditions in these parts many people residing in these areas having no work to earn their livelihood or those who find themselves in a difficult condition to maintain themselves naturally drift towards the urban areas with main objectives of eking out their livelihood. The relative advantage of the amenities available and job opportunities attract them towards big towns and cities and naturally there is a radical growth of inflow of poor and labour class to these cities and towns from all directions. So these people who have been pouring in almost continuously to the cities occupied unauthorized some vacant space in and around the cities with or without the help of their people and sometimes through some unauthorized agents or brokers or other vested interests.

2

Environment and Pollution

Environment is a fairly new concept and viewed with different angles by the human society. The word environment has been defined in a number of ways, for example—

(i) Environment is the sum of all social, economical, biological, physical and chemical factors, which constitute the surrounding of man, who is both creator and moulder of his environment.

(ii) Environment is the representative of physical components of the earth wherein man is the important factor influencing his environment. --*A. Goude*

(iii) Environment refers to the sum total conditions, which surround man at a given point in space and time. --*C.C. Park*

(iv) Environment is a holistic view of the world as it functions at anytime, with a multitude of special elemental and socio-economic systems distinguished by quality and attributes of space and mode of behaviour of biotic and abiotic forms.

It may be concluded that environment consists of an inseparable whole system constituted by physical, chemical, biological, social and cultural elements, which are interlinked individually and collectively in myriad ways.

Components of Environment

Any external force, material, circumstance or condition surrounding an organism and affects in any way are known as factors.

Costing has considered the environment as complex entity of variable factors, which include:

1. Matter — Land and Water.
2. Condition —Temperature and Light.
3. Force— Air and Gravity.

The various components of the environment has been divided into two categories as represented in the following table:

Table 1
Components of Environment

Biotic Components	*Abiotic Components*
1. Green and Leafy Vegetation	1. Air Water and Soil
2. Animal including man.	2 Energy and temperature
3. Micro-organism	3. Topography and gravity

Types of Environment

Environment is divided into two categories:

1). Natural Environment.

2). Anthropogenic Environment

The natural environment operates through self regulating mechanism, any change in natural ecosystem brought about by natural process is counter balanced by the opposing changes in the other components of the environment. These components include air, water, soil, land forest, wildlife, flora and fauna, etc. The environment has never been static and changes sometimes slowly and sometimes drastically which may be beneficial or harmful to living organisms. Many species in the biosphere could not adjust with changing environment, as a result of which they have been since vanished and many are on the brink of vanishing. The giant dinosaurs could not survive mainly because of some unfavourable conditions at that time.

Man, the most powerful environmental agent with his intelligence and initiative is capable of modifying the environment according to his need to a great extent by the application of modern technology and created an "Anthropogenic Environment" in the biosphere.

Segments of Environment

The environment is considered to compose of four different segments, which are—

(i) Lithosphere.

(ii) Hydrosphere.

(iii) Atmosphere.

(iv) Biosphere.

The lithosphere is mantle of rocks constituting the earth's crust. The soil contains mainly complex mixture of inorganic and organic matter and water, whereas hydrosphere includes all the surface and ground resources of water (oceans, seas, lakes, glaciers, polar ice caps, rivers, etc). The earth is called as the blue planet, because about 80% of the surface is covered by water.

However 97% of water resources are locked up in the oceans and seas, which are too saline for any human activities (drinking, agricultural, industrial, etc.), about 2.4% is trapped in glaciers and polar ice-caps and only 0.6% of the total world water resources are available for all human activities. Water exhibits unusual properties due to hydrogen bonding without which it would have boiled even at 100°C, in that case life on the earth would have been impossible. Because of hydrogen bonding, water is liquid at room temperature with melting point of 0°C and boiling point 100°C at normal atmosphere pressure.

The biosphere is the region of earth where all living and other organisms exit. It extends from about 10,000 metres below to 6,000 metres above sea level. The biosphere is an important segment of the environment as it covers the entire realm of living organisms and their interactions with the other segments.

The atmosphere comprises of mixture of various gases (nitrogen, oxygen, carbon dioxide, inert gases, etc.) in which, exchange of matter takes place between the atmosphere, biosphere and hydrosphere, their relative weights are in the following order-

Biosphere:	Atmosphere:	Hydrosphere
1:	300:	69,000

The atmosphere extends upto about 500 kms. Above the earth surface, surrounding the earth, acts as a gaseous blanket, protecting maintaining the heat balance, which keeps the earth warm enough to sustain life on the earth. Oxygen supports life, nitrogen is an essential micro-nutrient for plants and carbon-dioxide is essential for photosynthetic activity of plants. Apart from it, the atmosphere is a carrier of water from oceans to land.

Any major disturbance in the atmospheric composition by human activities may result in disastrous consequence endangering the very survival of living organisms on the earth.

The earth continuously receives energy from the sun, a part of which is absorbed, while remaining is emitted back into space. The heat balance is maintained within narrow limits, due to energy transfer process, which keeps optimum climatic condition for supporting life on the earth.

The quantity of solar energy per unit time passing through unit area at right angles to the direction of the solar rays measured just outside the atmosphere is called "Solar constant". The value of the solar 1400 watts/metre^2/minute and the heat equivalent is estimated to be 2.68x10^{24} joules/year. The 50 percent of which is reflected before reaching the surface of the earth, 15% is reflected by the earth's and evaporation of water on the surface of earth and the remaining 1.9% is absorbed by the marine, land and plant kingdom. The energy transfer plays a vital role in maintaining the radiation balance of the earth which proceeds through various mechanisms like conduction, convection, radiation and absorption.

Holocoenotic Concept on Environment

The environment consists of various biotic and abiotic components, which are quieting different but interrelated with each other. The living organisms present in the nature are affected each other. Thus, the all components of the environment are so intermingled with each other that neither can be separated nor transferred without affecting the other component, for example the increase in temperature results in decreasing humidity of the atmosphere, similarly increase in light intensity affects the photosynthetic process, temperature and humidity. It is quiet evident from the above that all the components of the environment are interdependent beside interrelationship. Sometimes it becomes too difficult to recognize that which component is responsible for a particular effect. This tendency of the joint effect of the components on the environments act and react between themselves constituting the environment yet it is a complete unit by itself.

Environmental Factors

The factors which affect the organisms are known as environmental factors. The organisms having more tolerance limit are largely distributed and can increase their number through re-productivity cycle operating in nature. These factors affect directly or indirectly the process of development and distribution of the organisms. The factors affecting the organisms are classified as:

A. Climatic Factors—These factors are subdivided into:

(i) Gases.

(ii) Humidity.

(iii) Light

(iv) Precipitation.

(v) Temperature.

(vi) Wind.

B. Topographic Factors—The following are the topographic factors:

(i) Altitude.

(ii) Direction of mountain chain.

(iii) Slope or Land.

C. Edaphic factors—These factors are:

(i) Soil Life.

(ii) Soil Profile.

(iii) Soil Temperature.

(iv) Soil Texture.

D. Biotic Factors—The factors influence organisms:

(i) Animals

(ii) Micro-organisms.

Multidisciplinary Nature of Environmental Studies

The study of environmental components is entirely a multidisciplinary in nature which includes all faculties like science, arts, commerce, meteorology, climatology, geography and other disciplines. The knowledge of all these branches is largely utilized for environmental studies.

In order to demonstrate the relationship of ecology with other faculties a cake of various layers can be imagined.

The horizontal division of the cake represents the basic divisions which are related to basic principles of all the living organisms and not with any particular species. Such as morphology, physiology, genetics, ecology, evolution, microbiology, etc., whereas the vertical divisions referred as "Taxonomic divisions" corresponding to the study of size, shape, activity and ecology of a particular community. It includes zoology, etc. The basic and taxonomic divisions are complementary to each other. The ecology is a branch includes the studies of abiotic environmental components besides the biotic components. In fact, it is quiet difficult to separate the ecology from other branches of sciences as it requires the knowledge of all aspects of anthropology, sociology, economics etc. To sum up it can be said that ecology is an 'Interdisciplinary Synthetic Science' and quiet important that is very difficult to determine the area, domain or limit and can be referred as 'Perennial sky'.

Scope and Importance of Environmental Science

Taylor in 1936 has stated that ecology is a science which includes the study of co-relationship between all the organisms with all the components of the environment. The study of ecosystem is present in nature with 'changing environment'. The function of ecology is to define the basic principles through which are various components of natural community function. The study of ecological principals is not limited to understand the relationship between natural communities and the environmental problems and to find a solution. The study also helps to access the damage to biotic and abiotic components of the environment as a result of establishment of a new undertaking at any place and to take necessary measures to compensate the loss. It is therefore, indisputable truth that the study of environmental problems, the technical society is facing today lies in correct understanding the concept of ecology and its application. Modern man, however, has initiated a number of abrupt changes during the last few centuries neglecting the concept of ecology resulting a general deterioration of the environment and disharmony in the world ecosystem which will lead quickly to catastrophic endangering the existence of organisms even man too. The development and continual availability of natural resources along with pollution free environment is only possible with better knowledge of ecology.

Pollution

The environment is a complex and dynamic system, in which all forms of life are inter-dependent and inter-connected. The basic amenities for living organisms are air, land or soil and water which were pure, virgin, undisturbed, uncontaminated in the past and basically most hospitable for living organisms present in the biosphere. The deterioration of environmental quality, which began when man first assembled in villages and utilized fire, thereafter rapid progress in further increased the problem. This has become as a serious problem since the industrial revolution and urbanization in the second half or the twentieth century. The environmental contamination of air, water, soil and food has become a threat to the continued existence of many plant and animal communities of the biosphere and might ultimately threaten the very survival of the human race.

Pollution of the environment is one of the most horrible ecological crises, which is usually brought about by the addition of waste products are not removed by the natural processes of the biosphere are accumulated and cause pollution. The rivers, seas, lakes, land or soil and atmosphere are polluted by wastes discharged by various industries, thermal power plants, exhaust of automobiles, fertilizers pesticides, insecticides, acidic rain, etc.

The most important and common pollutants are—

(i) Deposited Matters—Soot, smoke, tar, dust and fret

(ii) Gases—Carbonmonoxide, carbon dioxide, oxides ozone, ammonia, etc.

(iii) Chemical—Aldehydes, detergents, hydrogen fluoride, arsine, phosgene, etc.

(iv) Toxic metals—Cadmium, mercury, lead, iron, zinc, etc.

(v) Economic poisons—Herbicidies, pesticides, fungicides, insecticide, etc.

(vi) Fertilizers—Nitrogen, potassium, phosphorous, fertilizers

(vii) Sewage—Human waste, agriculture waste.

(viii) Radio active substance—Argon-41, cobalt-60, iodine-131, plutonium-239, etc.

(ix) Noise and Heat.

Types of Pollutants

The pollutants are classified as under

(1) Primary pollutants—The substances which are directly emitted from an identifiable source like oxides of sulphur and nitrogen are the primary pollutants.

(2) Secondary Pollutants—The substance derived from the primary pollutants by chemical reactions like peroxyacetyl nitrate are secondary pollutants.

The pollutants are also classified as biodegradable and non-biodegradable from eco-system point of view. The domestic sewage which can be easily decomposed is a biodegradable pollutant whereas present in the environment but added by anthropogenic activity, which do not degrade thereby pollute the environment. These pollutants not only accumulate but are often biologically magnified.

In general, pollutants are residues of substances made by man, used by man and even thrown away by man as waste products which pollute the environment. The society cannot survive if the natural environment collapses.

Pollutants need not be, material substances, however man is the principal source of pollution, because the nature is not capable to remove or decompose many man made materials and return to the cycle of nature. The pollution may be natural brought about by natural processes like forest fire, volcanic eruption, and earthquake or artificially due to human activities.

1. Classification According to Environment

There are two ways to classify the pollutants.

1. When different entities of the environment are affected by pollution, namely—

(i) Air Pollution

(ii) Water Pollution

(iii) Soil or Land Pollution

2. Classification According to the Pollutants

When the pollution is caused by pollutants like—

(i) Radioactive pollution

(ii) Sewage Pollution

(iii) Pesticide pollution

(iv) Noise pollution

(v) Thermal pollution

(vi) Plastic pollution

(vii) Marine pollution

(viii) Smoke and Smog pollution

(ix) Chemical pollution

(x) Industrial pollution

(xi) Drug pollution

(xii) Soap and Detergent pollution

(xiii) Oil pollution

(xiv) Oceanic pollution

(xv) Population

And many such due to human activities under the realm of civilization.

We pray to the Almighty to bestow his choicest blessings on the human society and guide to make the environment a green success so that all living organisms can lead a happy life and share the beauty of the earth.

Fundamental Principles of Pollution Control

The pollution controls methods are based on fundamental principles and aimed at cleaning up the environment so that the human hygiene, animals, forest are protected. The modern environmental movement has achieved much success but has also suffered many failures.

On the positive side is the fact that unprecedented support for environmental protection has developed, the public understands that the resources in land, fuels, raw materials, air and water are finite and must be protected and conserved. The technological society is doing many things to unbalance nature and to desecrate the environment that it is difficult to be selective. The people and problems are not yet clearly visible on the horizon. There are two ways, one is to learn and to live with the natural environment without destroying it and the second to eliminate the natural environment and create in its stead a sterile, chemical, technical world to serve man. Anyhow, the technology that has created manifold environmental problems is also cooperate with the nature because it will be a difficult option to go back to primitive age. The earth has got a unique property to conserve all the biotic components with all its resources.

Impact of Man on Environment

The impact of man environment through his varied and highly complex activities may be characterized as:

(i) Direct or intentional human activities are preplanned and man is aware of consequences. The effects of anthropogenic changes in the environment are noticeable with in short period and are reversible.

(ii) Indirect or Unintentional human activities are not preplanned and premeditated, the impacts arise from activities which are directed to accelerate the economic growth the industrial development. The indirect impacts are experienced after long time when they become cumulative.

Environmental Problems and their Types

Environmental problems created by anthropogenic activities in the name of development have effects like—

(i) Affecting human health, physiology efficiency, and general well-being, such as diseases, air and water pollution.

(ii) Detracting from the habitability of an area for example hazardous wastes and noise pollution.

(iii) Interference in the ecosystem, like thermal pollution, disruption of biogeochemical cycles, diversity.

(iv) Affecting the optimum use of resources such as soil erosion, water logging, salinization and alkalinization.

(v) Affect the entire biosphere, carbon-dioxide, ozone deflection, radiation balance etc.

Measures to Protect Environment

The measures suggested for the protection of environment are—

(i) Eco-friendly technologies should be used in the industries even at the loss of revenue. Strict law should be made and followed to reduce green house gases in the atmosphere. The technology must be developed for safer, more efficient and economical energy generation and utilization.

(ii) Forest should be developed near the industrial and mining areas because only good vegetation over the waste dump can prevent harmful nature of pollutants.

(iii) Technology should be developed for filtering of

industrial smoke and the harmful components may be absorbed in solvents as such the atmosphere remains safe for the living organisms.

(iv) Environmental safe energy should be adopted on large scale as the conventional energy sources contribute towards pollution.

(v) Public awareness programs should be run as most of the people hardly care of environmental pollution.

(vi) Above all, if we feel that "we did not inherit this world from our grand parents but we are borrowing it from our grandchildren".

Environmental Degradation

The major sources of environmental degradation are:

(i) Deforestation—It is a matter of serious concern that the modern man had forgotten the significance of natural vegetation which plays an important role in biospheric ecosystem. The forests have been environmental problems like floods, droughts, soil erosion, sediment load on the river, siltation, intensification of green house effect etc. The deforestation at global and regional level is due to population growth which require more land for habitation, agricultural, grazing land and form commercial activities etc.

(ii) Agricultural Development—It means expansion of agricultural land and increase in agricultural productivity. The use of technology, chemical fertilizers, more irrigation facilities, high yielding varieties of seeds, encroachment into forest land etc. has resulted increase in production of various crops to solve the food problem due to ever increasing world population. It has also created or is creating hazardous environmental problems of serious nature. The agricultural development degrades the environment in various ways through:

(a) Application of chemical fertilizers, pesticides and insecticides.

(b) Increase irrigation facilities and amount of irrigation.

(c) Changes in biological communities.

(d) Use of high yielding varieties of seeds affecting the carrying capacity of the land.

(iii) Industrial and Technological development—The industrial development has given economic prosperity but it has also created manifold environmental problems. The invention of productive technology in recent years to increase the productivity of industrial product is also closely related to the environmental crisis. The rapid rate industrialization along with productive technology has resulted into rapid rate of exploitation of natural resources.

Both the components of industrial development and production have created several lethal environmental problems and ecological imbalance at global, regional and local levels like:

(a) Reduction of forest covers for demand of land.

(b) Excavation of land for mining the minerals.

(c) Reduction in arable land for industrial expansion.

(d) Lowering water and polluting the water streams by discharging the industrial wastes.

(e) Collapsing ground surface due to mining activities.

(f) Releasing toxic gases into atmosphere. The Bhopal gas tragedy is an illustrative example of disastrous effect of modern industrialization.

The technology which is environmental friendly should be looked upon and at the same time stopping or at least reducing the use of technology which affects the environment adversely.

(iv) Population and Urbanization—The human population is growing at alarming rate because of better medical facilities and health care due to modern technology which is playing a significant role of lowering of environmental quality and ecological balance. More people require more food, more land for buildings, more minerals and more of everything to meet the unending demands of human society. Based on global average it has been calculated roughly that a city of one million inhabitants consumes about 625,000 metric tonnes of water, 2000 metric tonnes of food and 9500 metric tonnes of fuel. The larger cities also face the problems of air and noise pollution due to rise in number of personal vehicles and other means of transportation, for example the population of Jaipur the Pink City having a population approximately 15,97,774 and vehicles 9,807 in 1951 has now within a period of over 50 years the population has increase four fold whereas vehicles population from rural areas to urban and commercial centres are responsible for the environmental degradation and pollution. The problem was further exaggerated by unplanned plight, squatter settlements, lack of sanitation and water supply, overcrowding, congestion and pollution. A well controlled and well managed process of urbanization is necessary in order to check rural urban migration and other related problems.

(v) Consumerism—the development of civilization as a result of scientific innovation and technological advancements has led responsible for spreading the culture. The advertisements shown on different television channels and published in almost all news papers and magazines are so lucrative, fascinating, attractive and impressive that the people are beguiled and compelled to spent their earnings floated by many financial institution has further exaggerated the consumerism culture. In addition, the shopkeepers and manufactures do float schemes like purchase now, pay later, buy one and get one free, sure gift every purchase with bonus prize on scratch card, reduction of cost etc. have also added to consumerism

culture of society, over and above all that the established film stars, sports person do campaign the products though they might have not used those products and will not use in future also. It is just like adding 'Ghee into the Fire'. The people are infatuated and using all luxurious goods like air-conditioners, motor vehicles, mobile-phones, tinned foods, colour televisions etc. So much so the fruits, vegetables, flowers etc. of one's liking are being imported. There are several social repercussions of such changes in the basis and method of evaluation of social relations. The market mechanism and trade have changed maintenance of ecological balance of maximization of social benefits and maintenance of ecological balance to maximization of personal gains and raising production and revenue returns.

In the Present day Context

In the developmental and environmental degradation are two faces of same coin and go side by side. Despite this the society can neither ignore development nor afford to destroy the biosphere in which all kinds of organisms exist.

The general indifference of industries, on the aspect of environmental safety and protection along with the people who hardly care for environmental conservation if socio-political restrictions are not imposed. The urgency is of the 'environmental education' which can create environmental awareness among the people, increased efficiency and train specialists to tackle environmental problems.

It is quiet evident, the growing population, the present technology and consumerism culture are the main reason for environmental degradation will have to fight with two troublesome problems, depletion of natural resources and pollution of components of the environment to such an extent endangering the survival and existence of man. The pollution of water air and land by the human activities is described in short to understand the gravity of present situation.

A. Water—Water is known as 'Elixir of life'. It is the main support system of human life on earth. The substances which alter the physical, chemical and biological characteristics of water and cause harmful effects on living organisms are called the water pollutants. There are two basic sources of water pollution:

1. Natural sources which include soil erosion, land slide, volcanic eruption, decay and decomposition of plants and animals.

2. Anthropogenic sources are the real sources of water pollution which include industrial, urban, agriculture, cultural, sources, etc.

The most of the cities are situated on the banks of the rivers which supply water for all human activities but all these rivers are badly polluted by all types of wastes. The holy Ganga is highly polluted by approximately 1500 industrial units which are regularly discharging their effluents besides municipal wastes. The river Yamuna approximately carries 11000 quintals garbage and reaches Allahabad after travelling a distance of 1400 kilometres.

B. Air—The amount of nitric oxide is increasing in and around the industrial cities like Mumbai, Kolkata, Delhi, Kanpur, Ahmedabad, Agra, Hyderabad etc. It has been estimated that for every 8 tonnes of oxygen which has been utilized from the atmosphere, nothing has been added, instead 11 tonnes of carbon-dioxide is added into the atmosphere. Similarly with every new auto rolled off, the poisonous lead fumes are introduced in the atmosphere. The oxides of carbon, sulphur, nitrogen are increasing which result in acid rain and chlorofluoro-carbons promote green house effect and ozone depletion in the atmosphere.

C. **Land**—The land is polluted by the domestic and municipal wastes. Use and throw culture developed in the modern technological society is responsible for the collection of waste materials which are non-degradable in nature on the ground and pollute the air. The chemical fertilizers, pesticides and insecticides affect the fertility of land and agricultural products. The herbivorous animals as well as carnivorous animals are also affected on taking these products which has confirmed by the postmortem reports of the dead animals. The junks of domestic wastes and industrial wastes and industrial wastes like plastic bags, empty food cans, napkins, etc., are found in form of heaps, affecting the atmosphere and human health. Construction of dams, roads, canals and deforestation along with changes in cultivation practice do affect the characteristics of land

Environment in the Present Context

The Organism is a result of joint activities between the environment and genetics of the organism. The environment has much impact on the human health and activities. The pollution free environment provides better living conditions which are essential for healthy mind as health mind supports healthy body. It is quite necessary to keep the environment clean but the process of industrialization, urbanization and consumerism has affected the environment to a great extent. The development process influences the environment or in other words, the environment and development are interdependent. Relationship between man and environment has been point of discussion since the existence of man, but the perspective has now radically changed. Man on the pretext of development has turned from changer to transformer and now to destructor of the environment.

The human impact on the environment is direct function of patterns of use of natural resources and emission of pollutants into the biosphere and governed by the following factors.

(i) Quantity of natural resources consumed.

(ii) Amount of pollution generated per unit of output.

(iii) Output and consumption per capita.

(iv) Population size.

Enrich and Ehrlich put forwarded the following formula to describe the impact.

I =P x A x T

Where

I = Environment

P = Population Density

A = Per Capita Consumption

T = Harmful Technology used in production.

The environmental crisis is caused due to environmental and ecological changes as a result of developmental process. The present century is marked by socio-economic, scientific and technological development on one hand, it is plagued by serious problem of environmental degradation on the other hand. The environmental crisis arising out of the environmental deterioration caused by several forms of pollution, depletion of natural resources because of rapid rate of their exploitation and increasing dependence on energy consuming and ecologically damaging technologies, the loss of habitat due to industrial, urban and agricultural expansion, reduction and loss of ecological populations due to excessive use of toxic pesticides and herbicides and loss of several species of plant due to practice of mono-cultural removal of habitats through forest clearance has now become a global concern. The most striking reason for global environmental crisis is the fact of deteriorating relationship between man and the environment.

Ecology

The study of relationship between the living organisms

and the environments is ecology which is quiet important branch of science and it is not easy to find out the limits and domain or area of ecology. The ecology is helpful in understanding the following events:

(i) The mutual relationship between organisms and the environment.

(ii) The endemic and geographical distribution and abundance of organisms.

(iii) The regional characteristics of organisms and timely changes in their activities.

(iv) Adaptability of organisms with physical environment.

(v) The mutual relationship between the population and communities.

(vi) The developmental growth of mutual relationship.

(vii) The productivity of natural organisms and maximum production for the prosperity of mankind.

Sir Arthur Transley, a British Botanist put forward the concept of ecosystem in 1935 thereafter Eugenen P. Odum, an American Ecologist has defined the ecology as a "Study of natural anatomy and its functions". However Prof. P. Dudgeon of Allahabad University, Allahabad as early as 1921, has described the role of environment in communities succession. It was felt however in the middle of sixty to understand complexity and structure and working of various ecosystems operating in nature. The International Biological Programme (IBP) is the outcome of the thinking of world community. The importance was laid on biological productivity and prosperity of living organisms besides adaptively, utilization and conservation of resources in addition to estimation of productivity of terrestrial and aquatic ecosystem.

Through the international endeavour due to UNESCO organized 'Man and Biosphere' programme and United Nations Environment Conference held at Stockholm in 1972, emphasis has been made to conserve and judicious utilization of natural resources and world wide fund for nature has been contributed for the study of ecological aspect.

Branches of Ecology

The ecological study is carried on the following three angles of vision:

(i) Taxonomic Affinities—The communities like plants, animals, insects, micro-organisms, etc., are different but interrelated as such referred as organisms and study is carried our under the head of 'Plant Ecology' and 'Animal Ecology'

(ii) Habitat—On the basis of residence of various communities a new ecology 'Habitat Ecology' has emerged. The various forms are 'Forest Ecology' Grassland Ecology', 'Marine Ecology', 'Fresh Water Ecology', 'Desert Ecology', etc.

(iii) Level of Organism—From the viewpoint of ecology the level of organism or organization consists of either individual member of community or groups of communities as such subdivided into two categories.

a. Auto Ecology—The study of relationship of an individual specie with the environment is referred as auto ecology.

b. Synecology—It deals with the study of community groups present in the particular area and its relationship with the environment. The complex nature synecology has led further divisions which are:

(i) Population Ecology—It includes a group of single community.

(ii) Community Ecology—The study includes the different groups of a community which are interdependent and forms an unit of community.

(iii) Biome Ecology—The different community groups living in the area of similar climatic condition are known as biome. The different groups of community are inter-related. The mutual action between the different communities and environment is referred as biome ecology.

(iv) Ecosystem Ecology—It is a quiet new branch in which the biotic and abiotic components of nature remain in action with each other forming an ecosystem in which the study is carried out of biotic and abiotic components of each ecosystem and their mutual reacts.

In addition, phytogeography, Zoogeography, Gene-ecology, Production Ecology, Radiation Ecology, Space Ecology, Pollution Ecology, Human Ecology, Applied Ecology, etc., are also some of the important branches of ecological science.

Social Issues and the Environment

The growing population with limited natural resources and their irrational exploitation have resulted the environmental degradation. The United Nations has held conference in 1949 at Lake Sussex to discuss the problem of proper utilization and conservation of natural resources followed by the second conference in 1971 at Stockholm to consider the environmental problem. In the year 1992 'Earth Conference' was held at Rio-de-Janerio to discuss environmental degradation problem. The environment degradation is continuous process as such more than 150 pacts and agreements have been made on international level. The problem is much more related to social values and has great conscience amongst the people of 21st century. Today the world has accepted the ecology code of conduct and man has a right to live in proper natural environment. The environment has no boundary and any action in one part extends to all over the world.

The relationship between man and nature is an age old thing and the nature has given everything to man to fulfill his need. According to Mahatma Gandhi "Nature has enough to meet everyone's need but no one's greed" the technology which has made life more comfortable and pleasant by providing many such things which a primitive man might have not thought of even in his dreams. With the introduction of newer technology the man has affected his own environment to such an extent that he is helpless to restore it. The technology has no way to counter balance its action as the nature has capacity to sustain and counter balance the natural changes of the environment. The man should know about his environment and learn to live and co-operate with nature. Environmental studies and awareness given as idea about the importance and utility of natural environmental surrounding the biosphere sustaining the life. The man becomes more careful about his action of destroying the environment and solve environmental problem using his talent.

Unsustainable to Sustainable Development

The natural resources are affected by the human activities resulting in decrease in different quality of living organisms. It is therefore essential to decide that the development technique should be developed in such a way that the deterioration of environment should not obstructs the developmental activities. It has been accepted in principle that the environmental protection must be an essential part of the development. The solution lies to adopt the sustainable development programme and a committee was formed in 1984 under the chairmanship of the Prime Minister of Norway Mr. Brudland. The report entitled "Our Collective Future" has been published in 1987. The report has emphasized on the use of natural resources which are interdependent. The society did not inherit this wonderful world from the grandparents but have borrowed it from the grandchildren. This understanding amongst the people may however, help in the conservation of natural resources.

The land is a physical resource on which agriculture, forests, animal kingdom, etc., survive. The other natural resources are Air, Water, Energy, Nutrients, etc., which are quite important in their own way for the development of society. The man, is also included in the resources but due to his intelligence and skilled technique has utilized the other resources for his betterment. In the course of development, he has tried to produce, convert and transform these basic natural resources.

Social Problems

The exploitation of natural resources for the development affects the environment resulting many social problems. The limited natural resources specially land, air, water, energy are very much under pressure and are polluted by the passionate action and habit of human beings. Sky may not be a limit of development and science can provide all the things for leading a luxurious life but unable to add an inch of land, a litre of water or air. The social problems are as follows:

(i) Urban Problem—The modern development is city/ town oriented which has open ecosystem. There are biotic and abiotic components and social needs which require pure water, air, medical and health, housing and transportation facilities, sanitation, energy, social security, pollution free environmental, etc. The growing population of all the cities and towns has created problem and the existing infrastructure is not capable to accommodate the population and provide bare minimum need.

The noise, smoke, smell, etc. have now become the additional component of city environment which are responsible for pollution. The pollution level is regularly increasing and people are suffering from many ailments. The temperature has a tendency to increase because of large number of transportation vehicles and industrial complexes resulting the transformation of cities as hot islands.

(ii) Energy Problem—The energy is required for all domestic, commercial and industrial activities. Earlier the wood and coal were the prime source but cannot meet the present day requirement. The electric power has been used but there is much gap in demand and supply position as such energy crisis has erupted causing a serious problem. The home appliances like bulb, television, washing machine, heater, air-conditioner, geyser, etc. are commonly used by people as such demand has considerably increased. The power cut has affected the industrial activities to a great extent. The normal supply of electricity can only be maintained by producing more electricity by alternative methods like atomic power, hydroelectricity and use of natural gas. These sources may however be finished in due course of time therefore sources like solar energy, wind power and bio-gas plant have been suggested for additional energy requirement.

(iii) Drinking Water Problem—The water is quite abundant commodity present on the surface of earth but only about one percent water present in nature is available for human activities. Moreover the one percent ware source is fast depleting because of increasing population. The ground water level is also rapidly lowering down because of mass extraction and irregular and scanty rainfall. It is rightly pointed out that the next world war if at all happen will be due to drinking water problem.

The whole world is facing serious water shortage and requires suitable means to be adopted by the society to tackle the issue. The traditional method used by old generation and the neglected water sources should be considered to mitigate the problem. Watershed development programme has been developed which includes the traditional method together with the new techniques for sorting flowing water. The watershed management is supposed to solve the problem of water shortage to a great extent.

The process of urbanization of urbanization along with growing population have also contributed to water shortage. The water supply capacity of a town is not enough to meet the demand of water, than it is brought from another places through pipe lines which is many times is mixed with fifth due to leakage and broken pipe lines causing severe diseases.

(iv) Lack of Personal and Family Relationship—The growing population and development of civilization, the modern man has been faced with breaking of personal and family relations. The man being a social animal has a tendency to develop the personal relationship amongst the fellow members of the society. The means of transportation have brought persons from different parts and different family traditions to come closer in search of better living conditions but could not make harmony amongst themselves affecting the personal and family members used to participate in every functions. The people used to communicate their feelings through letters but with the advent of telephone and cards for every occasions, that personal touch has almost disappeared and has become a mere formality. In the process people have developed an indifferent attitude and have become self centred. The parents have no time for their own children who are brought up in different atmosphere away from family traditions because the joint family concept has almost vanished and children in hostels.

The all social values and traditions have thus become an outdated phenomena.

The problem is not only confined to family and personal relationship but also extended to social relationship as the school teaching at the childhood does not impart social, religions, cultural, etc., education but train students to operate computers, internet chatting, computer games, etc., under the pretext of modern and advanced education. The standard of general education has considerably fallen down.

No doubt, the revolution in transport means have brought the distant people closer to one another, the telecommunication revolution has separated the near relations apart.

(v) Resettlement and Rehabilitation Problem—The industrialization and urbanization have posed a great problem in the social structure of the society. The people from villages are migrating en masse to cities in search of better life. Secondly the increasing way of transportation, the people from remote and underdeveloped areas also migrating towards the industrially developed areas resulting a great pressure on land natural resources of the area.

The urbanization has resulted the housing problem causing inflation in price of urban-land. The rehabilitation and resettlement of people from the affected area is a matter of concern as of different culture, religion, habit are forced to live at one place in dwelling units having no facility for daily routine. There is a concept that the increasing number of 'Mammals' beyond a limit cause conflict between them. Social crimes, violence, tension, family conflict, rape, intoxication, etc. are the result of urbanization and industrialization. The only way to control and cheque these social problems to make awareness amongst the people, if once it is awaken the all constructive dimension will open itself.

3

Environmental Protection Acts

In the primitive age of human civiiization, the man was in the state of nature and the first feeling was that of hunger and self preservation. Man is both creator and moulder of his environment. He has acquired power to transform his environment in countless ways and on an unprecedented ways through the rapid acceleration of science and technology. To make living and enjoying life man used the nature, but unfortunately, the same was abused. In that process water, food, land and air were used indiscriminately affecting the dynamics of plant and animal life on earth by altering ecological balance. The balance in ecology is the same as equilibrium in nature governed by natural law which upholds the harmony or proportion in nature.

Environmental Ethics

It was religion in earlier days which was guiding the development of human society in general and individual in particular. The people by and large had accepted it as a sacred duty to observe and act accordingly to religious ritual. The science and religion were complementary yet religion had dominated.

All major religions have categorically pointed out that the man is a part of biospheric ecosystem and all components of biosphere viz., air, water, land, plant and animal including man are interdependent; mutually reactive and interconnected with their physical environment on one hand and among themselves on the other hand. Man being a part, also depends on the continued functioning of biosphere for his own existence. All most all religions treat nature as a God given gift. Some even stating that all mighty God is omnipresent in the manifestations of nature.

Religion and Environment

It is pertinent to examine the religious thoughts in the context of environmental and human relationship.

(i) Hindu Religion and Environment—The Hindu religion is one of the oldest religion of the world. Ever since Vedic times, the main motto of social life was to have in harmony with the nature and considered space, air, fire, water and earth as *'Panchbhuta'* (five elements) and worshipped. It was regarded as sacred duty of the mankind to protect them. According to mythology, the space *(Akasha)* was first creation of Brahma, Aakash created air, *(vayu)* and *vayu* produced fire (*agni*). The water (*Jal*) and earth (*Prithvi*) are later creations. These five elements have been regarded as Lord Surya or Agni Devta; Sun (God of Fire); Vayu Devta (Lord of Air); Varuna Devta (Lord of Water); Akash (abode of Devtas); Prithvi (Mother Earth) and worshipped accordingly.

India had been most advanced country of the world at that time as the Indians were quite aware of nature and ecological equilibrium. The religious books like Rigveda, Atharveda regarded the plants and animals have divine power which are indispensable in the life of human being and associated them with various Gods and Goddesses. The following tables list some of the names of trees and animals associated with Gods and Goddess.

Table 1

Trees and Abode of Gods/Goddesses

S. No.	*Tree*	*Associated Gods/Goddesses*
1.	Ashoka	Buddha, Indra
2.	Fig	Vishnu, Rudra (Shiva)
3.	Kadamb	Krishna
4.	Lotus	Laxmi
5.	Mango	Laxmi, Goverdhan
6.	Neem	Sitala, Manasa
7.	Palasa	Brahma, Gandharva
8.	Pipal	Krishna, Vishnu
9.	Vat (banyan)	Brahma

Table 2

Animals Associated with Gods and Goddesses

S. No.	*Animals*	*Associated God/Goddesses*
1.	Ass	Sitla
2.	Bull, serpent and Snake	Shiva
3.	Crocodile	Ganga
4.	Deer	Vayu
5.	Dog	Bhairava (an incarnation of Shiva)
6.	Eagle	Vishnu
7.	Elephant	Indra and ganesh
8.	Fish	Karma
9.	Lion	Durga

10.	Monkey	Rama and hanuman
11.	Owl	Laxmi
12.	Peacock	Karthikeya and Saraswathi
13.	Rat	Ganesh
14.	Swan	Saraswathi
15.	Wild goose	Brahma

It is quite evident that Hindu religion prohibits cutting and killing of these of trees and animals since a long time and happens to be concept of way of life having deep faith In the doctrine of *Ahimsa* (non-violence). It has preached not to cut and kill the God's creation but to protect.

By the end of Vedic and Upanishadic periods Buddhism and Jainism concepts have developed in India which have also insisted on non-violence, truth, respect, and love for all the living organisms. These religions also continued to conserve and protect the natural resources. Ashoka, the great emperor of India who adored Buddhism after Kalinga war promoted the plantation and preservation of flora and fauna and prescribed serious punishment for the killing animals and cutting trees. Similarly 'Ahimsa' has been accepted as the foundation of the Jains, some of them are known as *Karmdan,* viz., *Vankarm, Sphotrk Karm, Nirlanchen Karm* and *Asatipashan Karm* which are related to the environment. Sikhism (*Khalsa Panth*) also emerged as a school of religious thought in the recent times, which has also laid emphases of protecting and enriching the natural environment. In *Gurunanak Bani* (religious discourse) the term *Jaga* and *Jagat* refer to the world and convey the ideas of process of creation from water. Fire and air and the God is the creator of these. In the modern India, Bankim Chandra has pronounced sacred verse 'Vande Matram' in the honour of mother earth.

(ii) The other religions of the world like Islam, Parsi,

Christianity, etc. also respect the nature and instruct their followers to conserve and protect it. The God has created the earth and implanted therein hills, mountains, valleys, rivers, forests and the plains wherein dwell animals, birds and other living creatures and all these are for the service of man, for his use, enjoyment, sustenance and development but he should remember that other living creature also have a right to exist. According to Quran, the owner of land on this earth is God and whosoever is in-charge, possession or control thereof is only a trustee and all are beneficiaries of nature. The Christians believe that 'The earth is a blessing and a Trust of the Lord and we must preserve it with all our might: The Parsi religion also worships fire as 'Aagyaari!'.

It is amply clear from above description that the natural resources and human beings are the creation of one superior power and each one of them is dependent on one another. Destruction and damage to any is the destruction of self. One is complimentary to the other as such interdependence, co-operative living and close association with other components of environment is the real basis of human existence.

Environment and Technology

The aesthetic sense due to the religious teaching remained main driving force till industrial revolution, which took place in Britain and European countries and spreaded all over the world. The science and technology has slowly and gradually made head away and overpowered the religion. The religion, no doubt gives the spiritual strength and peaceful atmosphere, the science and technology have provided the physical charms which led to unrest in the society and provided the people to get more and more by any means at any cost. The paradoxical situation in which rapid scientific and technological changes have been associated with the rapid destruction of mankind. The continued degradation of environment is the result of modern living, technological advancements, industrialization and urbanization. The scientific and industrial revolution has significantly transformed the relationship between the man and the nature. It has rightly been said that man is nature's best promise and worst enemy. The society has now guided missile and misguided man. With scientific knowledge, man is able to transform deserts into oasis, he is also leaving behind deserts in the place of oasis. It is a tragedy that the new world has been created on the grave of the old world which lived in harmony with nature.

The rapid economic development, technological and scientific advancements have destroyed the natural environment and by now it should be clear that the environment is becoming less capable of sustaining the growing impact of the economic development. The people who still advocate the old principles are called backward and the new generation running fast to get all the worldly charms, headings fast for extinction. "Make no haste. You would reach early to destination", it is therefore, to avoid the major catastrophic or extinction of mankind due to environmental pollution which has become so acute that it is quite difficult even to diffuse. The environmental pollution is the worldwide phenomena. According to a report there is 28 percent increase in death rate due to pollution in 1995 in comparison to 1991. There are 10,647 deaths in Kolkatta, 9859 in Delhi and 7022 in Mumbai in 1995 and about 2.6 crores of people are affected by pollution every year in India. The age old environmental ethics to live in harmony with nature is almost a forgotten past.

Public Awareness

The people have now realized and have become aware about the environment. The United Nations Organization have organized a conference in 1949 at Lake Sussex to draw attention towards the early destruction of natural resources. The U.N. Conference on the Human Environment held at

Stockholm from June 5 to June 16, 1972, has been regarded as first major attempt to solve the global problem of conservation and regulation of human environment by international agreement at universal level.

(i) The Declaration on the Human Environment—The declaration consists of two parts; the first part proclaims seven truths about the man in relation to the environment and the second part enunciates 26 principles. The concept of 'Sustainable Development' was mooted by U.N. World Commission on Development and Environment (1987) which means development that meets the needs of present generation without compromising the ability of future generation to meet their own need.

(ii) Earth Summit, 1992—The earth summit under the auspices of United Nations was held at Rio de Janeiro, from June 3 to June 12, 1992. It was largest International Conference in the history of International relations and International law; approximately 20,000 participants of 178 Nations and 130 Heads of State Governments participated in the summit.

Rio de Janeiro declaration contains 27 principles concerning almost all countries of the global community and enlisting general rights and obligations on environmental protection. The Rio de Janeiro summit is a milestone which has pointed a direction of hope for both the developed and under-developing nations to bring it to fruitation so as to ensure the world is safe for the present and future generations.

(iii) Environmental Conservation and Need for Public Awareness—Most of the countries of the world are suffering from many problems amongst them and all are related to the environmental pollution. Every nation is facing the problem of maintaining a healthy atmosphere in continuation for ever for all the times. The problem is not concerned to individual and all is necessary to get rid to the problem of the environmental pollution. There are some suggestions which should be followed and implemented seriously in order to save the environment for further deterioration and conserve the natural resources available and use them without over-exploitation. The suggestions are:

(i) Change the consumerist tendency.

(ii) Afforestation in rural areas.

(iii) Avoid excessive use of self driven auto.

(iv) Encourage mass transportation system in big cities.

(v) Manufacturing of plastics and such non biodegradable compounds be stopped completely.

(vi) Development of feeling of coexistence between the environment and the men.

(vii) Introduction of environmental education in schools.

(viii) Promoting traditional ritual at the childhood stage for conservation.

(ix) Equitable use of resources for sustainable development.

The life cycle on earth may continue forever and may lead a peaceful life. It is necessary for the present generation to use the natural resources economically and wisely. The life style should be oriented towards the perpetual values. The daily routine of a person should be closer to nature and support and not to destroy nature. In short the life style of the man should be such that it conserve the natural resources and the action of him should not prove disaster to the environment.

(iv) Society and organization for Environmental Conservation—There are thousands of organizations which are associated with the conservation of environment in India, more than 100 such organizations are local, state wise, National and International level which are engaged in research, training, education and making awareness amongst the people. A shortlist is given as under:

A. International Organizations

1. Friends of the Earth.
2. Green Peace
3. International Biological Programme
4. United Nations Environment Programme
5. World Conservation Monitoring Center.
6. World Conservation Unit.
7. World Wildlife fund.

B. National Societies

1. Bhartiya Wild Life Organization, Dehradun.
2. Bombay Natural History Society, Mumbai.
3. Ecological Research and Training Center, Bangalore.
4. Environmental Education Centre, Ahmed Nagar.
5. Govind Ballabh Pant Himalayan Environment Development Organization, Almora.
6. Ministry of Environment and Forest, New Delhi.

Environmental Protection Act

In earlier days, the sages, saints and great teachers were very close to the nature. They have preached the people to use the resources available wisely and economically, and conserve and do not pollute the sources. Those preachers were wise enough to give religious touch to their scientific observations. Knowing well that the man is weak by nature and religion would stop him to destroy the ecosystem stability. This prevailed for a long time. The people struggled for a long time for a better way of life and could achieve through the development of science and technology which overcome the religious bent of mind and diverted it to worldly pleasure. During the process, the natural resources have been overexploited and environmental degradation took place with a faster speed. The environment which could sustain for many centuries have been exploited and polluted during the first few decades of twentieth century to the extent that the survival and even existence of living organisms has become a matter of great concern.

Many attempts have been made by individual, social workers, societies and organizations to tackle the problem of environmental degradation and pollution bur remained futile because of non-participation of people and absence of any law to take suitable measures for punishment to defaulters. The global concern has been found and but no concrete steps were found visible as the people by and large neglected the principles laid down by the convention held in 1992 at Rio de Janeiro under the auspices of United Nations. The people were now guided by science and technology rather than by religion on the environmental issues.

The environment issues were incorporated in the Indian Constitution by the 42nd Amendment which was passed in 1977. The Article 48A has given the responsibility to the center and state governments to protect and conserve the environment whereas Article 51A(g) has made people responsible to contribute for the improvement of environment. The environmental laws have been framed to protect and improve the environment and to protect and control any act or omission of polluting or likely to pollute the environment. There are about five hundred laws in India directly or indirectly which are subject matter of legislation which did not find place in the Indian law books until as late as 1974, has enacted.

There are more than 200 articles concerning the

environment which can be classified under the following heads.

Structural Basis of Environment Laws

Protective Laws		**Planning Laws**	
For Human being	*For Non- human being*	*For Production*	*For Distribution*
Air	Flora	Catchment area	Biosphere
Noise	Marine life	Estuaries	Housing
Nuclear	Wild Life	Grazing land	Land ceiling
Radiation		Industry	Parks
Toxic		Irrigation	Recreational areas
Water		Land utilization	Sanctuaries
		Mining	Slums
		Waste land	Town planning

Some of the acts listed below

1. The Mines and Mineral (Regulation and Development) Act, 1947.
2. The Factory Act (Pollution and Pesticides), 1948.
3. Damodar Valley Corporation (Water Pollution Control) Regulating Act, 1948.
4. The Industries Development and Regulation Act, 1951.
5. The River Board Act, 1956.
6. The Prevention of Food and Adulteration Act, 1954.
7. The Municipality Act, 1959.

8. The Bidi and Cigar Control Act, 1961.
9. The Rajasthan Noise Control Act, 1961.
10. The Insecticide Act, 1968.
11. The Atomic Energy Act (Radiation Protection Rules), 1971.
12. The Wildlife (Protection) Act, 1972 (Revised in 2002).
13. The Water (Prevention and Control of Pollution) Act, 1974 (Revised in 1988).
14. Forest (Conservation) Act, 1980 (Revised in 1988).
15. Air Pollution (Prevention and Control) Act, 1981 (Revised in 1987).
16. Environmental (Protection) Act, 1986.

The details of some of the acts are described below:

Environment Protection Act, 1986

As a sequel to Stockholm conference on the human environment in June 1972, an amendment was made in the constitution of India introducing Article 48A and 51A (Fundamental duties). Later on, the Government enacted the 'Environment Protection Act' in 1986, to provide for the protection and improvement and prevention of hazards to human beings, other living creatures, plants and property. Though there are laws dealing directly or indirectly with several environment matters, there was no general legislation for environmental protection.

The President of India has granted permission to the Act on 23rd May, 1986 and was published in Gazette on 26th May, 1986. The Act came into force since 19th November 1986. The act has empowered the Central Government for the comprehensive control of environmental pollution by the industrial and related activities of man.

The act is framed in 4 chapters and 26 sections:

6A-1. Chapter 1: It contains two sections

Section 1: It includes short title, extent and commencement.

Section 2: The definitions of

(i) Environment.

(ii) Pollutants.

(iii) Environmental Pollution

(iv) Handling

(v) Hazardous substances.

(vi) Occupier (person)

(vii) Prescribed by the rules under the act

The emphasis in the act is laid down on the physical condition of air and water. The major urban environmental problems like noise, traffic, mass transportation system, slums and congestion are not included in the Act. There is much ambiguity in definitions which can be interpreted in either way which tends to restrict control over harmful substances. It is purely a jugglery of technical words.

Chapter 2: It contains 4 sections in which the general power granted to the Central Government to take all the measures for protecting and improving the quality of the environment and for preventing, controlling and abating environmental pollution.

The Central Government is also empowered to constitute one or more authorities for exercising and performing all such of the powers and functions of the Central Government under the Act that can be specified.

In addition to above, the other powers endowed to the Central Government are:

(a) Appointment of Officers—Under the section 4. The Central Government is empowered to appoint officers for the purpose of the legislation. The authorities and officers shall work under the supervision, direction and control of Central Government.

(b) Power to give Direction—Section 5 gives power to the Central Government, in exercising its powers and performance to instruct in writing any person, officer or authority including closure, prohibition, operation or process, stoppage of supply of electricity, water or any other services. The instructions issued are obligatory and cannot be ignored.

(c) Power to Frame Rules—Section 6 of the act empowers the Central Government to reduce or control the pollution. The rules so framed under section 3 will be notified through Official Gazette, which would be related to:

(i) The standards of quality of air, water and soil for various areas and purposes.

(ii) The maximum allowable limits of concentration of pollutants including noise for different areas. For noise pollution apart from areas timings can also be included.

(iii) The procedure of handling and safeguarding measure of hazardous substances.

(iv) The prohibition and restriction of shorting hazardous substance in different areas.

(v) The restriction on the location of the industries and operation in different areas.

(vi) The procedure and safeguard to avoid accidents leading to pollution and make remedial measures for any such mishap.

(d) Powers to Delegate—Under the section 23 of the Act the Central Government may delegate few powers to

State Government any officer of authority. Accordingly, the Central Government by notifying through Official Gazette such conditions and parameters by delegating the powers to take any action which is necessary but cannot frame any rules. The main objective is for successful implementation of the Act. It is not out of place to mention that the delegated authority is not fully disowned from powers (Judgment of Patna high Court, Ramsingh v/s State of Bihar, 1979, B.L.J.R.,496.)

6A-3. Chapter 3- Prevention control and abatement of environmental pollution:

It lays out the substantive provisions relating to prevention, control and abatement of pollution. The provisions are:

(i) Section 7 of the Act restricts any industry or person during operation or process shall discharge or emit or permit to be discharged or emitted, any pollutant above the permissible standards.

(ii) The section 8 of the Act binds a person to handle or cause to be handled any hazardous substance in accordance with only such procedures which are presented as safeguarding measures.

(iii) The section 9 of the Act enjoins upon certain persons to furnish information to authorities and agencies regarding any accidents, unforeseen event, death etc. on account of excessive discharge of environmental pollutants above the prescribed standards. The person responsible for discharge of pollutants in excess of prescribed standards is bound to prevent or mitigate the pollution and must report to government and render all possible help on demand. The person concerned is also liable to pay the amount with interest on the treatment by agency as decided by government (Vide section 3 subsection 2).

The above provision in Act provides sufficient arrangement for protection and abatement of pollution and assign responsibility to human society, governments and individual person to perform their duty of protection and improvement of the environment.

Power to enter, inspect, take sample etc.—The section of this Act delegates the power of entry and inspection by any person appointed by Central Government who will have the right to enter in the premises of industrial and commercial establishments at all reasonable times for the purpose of performing any functions entrusted to him. According to the section 11 of the Act, the person has the power to take sample of air, water and soil or other substances from any factory, premises or other places for analysis in such manner as may be prescribed. The provision of section 11 relating to sampling is very much like the one in Prevention of Food Adulteration Act, which is lawyer's paradise. The provision has a tendency to protect the guilty rather than the environment.

Environmental Laboratories—The Act provides that the Central Government may be by notification in the Official Gazette, establish environmental laboratories and recognize one or the more to laboratories or institutes as the environmental laboratories to carry out testing and some functions as may be prescribed under the Act. In addition to this, the person having the prescribed qualifications may be recognized as Analyst for the purpose of analysis of sample of soil, water and air or other substances sent to environmental laboratories.

Legal Provisions for Penalties—The Act provides for the severe penalties and punishments as under:

(a) Any person who fails to comply with or contravene any of the provisions under the Act or the rules, orders, or directions issued under the Act shall be punished for each failure or contravention with a prison term of 5 years or a fine upto Rs. 1 lakh or both. The Act further imposes an additional fine of upto 5000 rupees for every day of continuing violation. In case of failure or contravention occurs for more than once after the date of first conviction, the offender may be punished with the prison term which may be extended to seven years.

(b) Offences by Companies—Any offence under this Act has been committed by a company, every person, who at the time of offence has directly in-charge and responsible to the company for the conduct of the business of the company, and the company itself shall be deemed to be guilty of the offence and shall be liable to be prosecuted. During the proceedings if it is proved that the offences was committed with the consent or connivance of any director, manager, secretary or other officer of the company they shall also be deemed liable to be proceeded against accordingly.

The Act provides all the persons to be proceeded which is not fair at the first sight to proceed all the partners of the firm as all of them may not even be knowing what has really happened but sometimes, it is essential to go to the root cause and truth of the events that has happened.

Offence by the Government Department—Any department of the Government, the head shall be deemed to be guilty of the offence and shall be liable to be proceeded against unless he proves that the offence has committed without his knowledge or he exercised all due diligence to prevent the happening of the offence as per section 17 of the Act.

The loopholes provided in sections 16 and 17 to get of the hook or proof of lack or knowledge or due diligence also dilute the effect of panel provisions.

6A-4. Merits of the Act

(i) The Act has defined the dangerous industrial activities and environmental disasters.

(ii) The Act has not been confined to water and air only but also has been extended to include all environmental pollutants.

(iii) The Act has provided server punishment to prevent the environmental pollution.

(iv) The Act has provided extreme powers to the Central Government to direct and closure of pollution causing establishments, even the government organization have also been included under Article 213 of the Act.

6A-5. Weakness of the Act

(i) All powers have been delegated to the Central Government, which restricts quick action.

(ii) The punishment provisions are not in accordance to the activities of big business houses.

(iii) Issuances of 2 months notice to public interest petition in accordance to general concept.

(iv) The constitutional standards for the companies are very less.

(v) The deforestation, ecological dis-equilibrium and atomic energy establishments have not been included.

6A-6. Conclusion—Inspite of several defects in the Act, the objectives of environment protection and conservation can be achieved if the principles and spirit of the Act are seriously and effectively implemented by the authorities, because no civil court is having jurisdiction to entertain any suite or proceedings in respect of anything done, action taken or order/direction issued by the Central Government or any other authority or officer in pursuance of any powers conferred on them in this Act. (Section 22 of the Act).

6B. The Air (Prevention and Control of Pollution) Act 1981 (Amended in 1987)—This Act was passed by the Indian parliament on 29th March in the exercise of its power conferred and came into force since 16 May, 1981. The Act was amended in 1987.

6B-1. Objective of the Act—The Act was framed on the suggestions made in the 'Human Environment' Conference held in 1972. It is legislative attempt to control the air pollution, which is part of the environmental pollution. The main objectives of the act are:

(i) To make provision for the control, prevention and relieving the air pollution.

(ii) To establish the Central and State Boards for controlling air pollution.

(iii) To make provisions for the above subject.

6B-2. The Constitution of the Act—The Act has 7 chapters and 57 sections.

Chapter 1. Preliminary

Chapter 2. Central and State Boards

Chapter 3. Power and Functions of Boards

Chapter 4. Prevention and Control of Pollution

Chapter 5. Penalties and Procedure

Chapter 6. Power of State Government to supersede State Boards

6B-3. Salient Features of Sections of the Act—

(i) The Act provides that the Central Pollution Control Board, which has constituted under Section 3 of the Water (Prevention and Control) Act of 1974, has been delegated powers to function as the 'Central Pollution Control Board' for the prevention and control of air pollution and new board has been constituted for the purpose. The Central Board shall also exercise the powers and perform the functions of the State Boards in Union Territories.

(ii) Section 2 defines the terms air pollution in detail.

(iii) Section 5 empowers State Governments to constitute the State Boards which shall be a body corporate with the name specified by the State Government in the notification issued under Sub-Section (1). The Board has been declared as a 'legal person as it can acquire and dispose off property and may sue and be sued as the State Board. However, the State Government can withdraw powers vide section 47 and 48 in emergency.

(iv) To establish the standard for wastes and effluents discharged from industries. (Section 20)

(v) According section 21(1) no industry can be established without permission of the Board in the air pollution control areas.

(vi) The Board is authorized to:

a. Inspection of any industry. (Section 24)

b. Selection of factory. (Section 26)

c. Analysis of samples. (Section 26 to 29)

d. To decide the penalty. (Section 37 and 39)

(vii) According to Section 43, no civil court take notice of any of the Sections in normal conditions.

6B-4. Chief Characteristics of the Act:

(i) It is applicable throughout India

(ii) State government can declare any areas as "Air Pollution Control Area" and all the establishments situated in the area shall have to obtain. 'No Objection Certificate' and permission from the State Board for their activities.

(iii) The Board is empowered to issue instructions regarding the pollutants and can exercise power for closure and cut electricity and water supply to the establishment.

(iv) No person can suite file directly to industry for not following the provisions of the act

(v) The State Government can repeal, turndown and keep in abeyance any decisions of State Boards.

6C. The Water (Prevention and Control of Pollution) Act 1974—(Amended in 1988): This Act has become effective since 23rd March, and applicable now throughout the country.

6C-1. Object of the Act—The main aim and object of the Act is to maintain and restore the wholesomeness of water and to prevent, control and abate water pollution.

6C-2. Constitution of the Act—There are 8 Chapters and 64 Sections in the Act—

Chapter 1: Preliminary. (Section 1-2)

Chapter 2: Constitution of Central and State Boards. (3-12)

Chapter 3: Constitution of Joint Boards. (13-15)

Chapter 4: Powers and Functions of Boards. (16-18)

Chapter 5: Prevention and Control of Water Pollution. (19-32)

Chapter 6: Funds, Accounts and Audits. (34-40)

Chapter 7: Penalties and Procedures. (41-50)

Chapter 8: Miscellaneous. (51-64)

6C-3. Chief Sections of the Act—

(i) Section 1 has defined occupier output, pollution, sewage, effluent, sewer stream, trade effluent; Central

Board vide various sub sections.

(ii) Section 3 and 4 have given direction for the construction of Central and State Boards respectively.

(iii) Section 13 has laid down provisions for the constitution of Joint Boards of Central and State Governments.

(iv) Section 20 has mentioned about the powers for collecting information.

(v) Section 21 has empowered the Boards to collect samples for many establishments.

(vi) Sections 24-27 have provided the measures for controlling water pollution.

(vii) Sections 42-44 have provisions for penalizing the people and establishments who are not observing the pollution standards of water.

(viii) Sections 51-52 refers to the establishments of water establishment of 'Water Testing Laboratories' by the Central and State Governments.

(ix) Sections 53-54 refers to the analysis procedures

6C-4. Chief Characteristics of the Act:

(i) To make water free from pollution and restoration to its initial stage.

(ii) A detailed terminology regarding water pollution has been prepared and defined.

(iii) The different sources of water have been included

(iv) A comprehensive program has been chalked out on the principles of 'Permit System' and 'Consent Procedure'

(v) Necessary permission is to be sought before establishing an industry

(vi) Provision of severe punishment and penalties to pollution making agency

(vii) Provision of 'General Public Writ Petition'.

6D. the Wildlife (Protection) Act 1972, (Amended in 1991)

The Indian parliament has passed the Act on 9th September 1972 which has proved to be a milestone in the direction of conservation of wildlife because it has brought the wildlife protection under the contiguous list which was earlier a subject of state jurisdiction. The Constitutional Article 249, 250 and 250 have empowered the Central Government to protect the wildlife. The wildlife act is applicable throughout the country except Jammu and Kashmir.

6D-1. the Objects and Features of the Act—

(i) To make sure the conservation and management of wildlife.

(ii) To ban hunting of animals and business relating to skin and skin products of wildlife.

(iii) Compulsory vaccination of all animals living in 5 kilometres vicinity of 'National Parks' and 'Sanctuaries'.

(iv) To arrange necessary facilities and strengthen the management of 'National Parks' and Sanctuaries'.

a. Control measures of poaching of animals

b. Captive breeding of endangered species.

c. Development of Zoo.

d. Wildlife education to public.

(v) Complete ban on activities like ignition of fire, carry of fire arms explosives and any harmful material in sanctuaries, national parks and zoo.

(vi) The defaulters shall be penalized with 3-5 years of imprisonment or Rupees 5-25 thousand or both as penalty. To kill the 'National Bird' peacock the terms of imprisonment is upto 10 years.

6D-2. Constitution of the Act—The act has seven chapters six schedules and 66 sections. The wildlife animals have been classified into six schedules:

Chapter 1: preliminary. (Section 1-2)

Chapter 2: Authorities to be appointed/constituted (3-8)

Chapter 3: Hunting of wild animals (9-17)

Chapter 3A: Protection of specified plants (17A-17H)

Chapter 4: Sanctuaries, National Parks and Closed Areas (18-38)

Chapter 4A: Constitution of Central Zoo Authority (38A-38J)

Chapter 5: Trade or Commerce in Wild Animals (39-49)

Chapter 5A: Prohibition of Trade and Commerce in trophies, Animal articles, etc. (49a-49C)

Chapter 6: Procedure and detection of offences (50-58)

Chapter 7: Miscellaneous (59-66)

6D-3. Principal Sections of the Act:

This Act was passed and implemented on 23rd October 1980 and amended in 1988. The act has jurisdiction all over the country except Jammu and Kashmir.

6E-1. Objects of the Act—The main objectives are:

(i) To prevent deforestation and to check ecological imbalance.

(ii) To apply the provisions of all type of forests.

(iii) To acknowledge the forest as renewal natural resources rather than earning source.

(iv) To discourage the utilization of forest land for miscellaneous purposes.

(v) To regularize the encroachment of forest land by poor landless tribal persons.

6E-2. Constitution of the Act—The amended act has five sub-divisions:

(i) Extent and commencement

(ii) Restriction or de-reservation of forest land for non forest purposes.

(iii) Constitution of advisory committees.

(iii-a-b) Punishment—to government and officers for violation

(iv) Power to make rules.

(v) Repeal and Saving

6E-3. Salient Features of the Act—

(i) To withdraw the power of the State Governments for utilizing the forests land for non-forest purposes.

(ii) To constitute the advisory committee for advising the Central Government for the conservation of forest.

(iii) To stop immediately any type of activity damaging the forest.

(iv) To give necessary permission for the developmental works like constructions of roads, dams, laying out of electricity poles, mining etc. The permission is granted with few conditions and the transfer of forest land for the above mentioned work can be made.

(v) Violations of provisions and conditions by the offender would be punished by the competent court, even the Government officer can be imprisonment for 15 days.

7. Conclusion

In order to save all the segments of environment and the provide a clean, healthy and pure pollution free environment for better human life, the above five Acts have been described to make awareness in general pubic. The people must be educated by the provisions of the Acts. It is the duty of the people to work in accordance with spirit of the acts and mould the life style and bring necessary changes. The work is for collective benefits and collective bright future for one and all.

4

India and Its Ecosystem

The Indian subcontinent occupies a strategic position in southern Asia. It is favourably situated on the world's highways of trade and commerce both to the east and the west stretching 3,214 kilometres from north to south between the extreme latitudes and 2,933 kilometres from east to west between the extreme longitudes, India covers a land area of 32,87,263 square kilometres constituting 2.42 percent of earth's surface. India supports 16.7 percent of the world's population and 20 percent of the cattle of the world.

Bio-geographical Classification of India

India is a large subcontinent where variety of vegetation, land structure, climate, etc. exist. The different kind of flora and fauna from alpine to equatorial types are found in India with wide range of temperature variations. The main land consists of four well defined regions:

i) The great mountain zone

ii) The Indo-Gangetic plain

iii) The desert region

iv) The Southern peninsula

Apart from mainland there are about 247 islands and of which 220 islands are situated in Bay of Bengal. The principal islands are.

(1) Andaman and Nicobar in Bay of Bengal—The northern cluster of islands consist of 201 islands is called Andaman and the southern cluster of 19 islands is known as Nicobar.

(2) The Lakshadweep in Arabian Sea—Comprise a group of 27 coral islands out of which 17 islands are uninhabited.

India as a Mega-diversity Nation

There is a great biodiversity and the country has been classified in nine regions on the basis of tree and plant kingdom.

A. The Western Himalayas

B. The Eastern Himalayas

C. The Indus Plains or Western Deserts

D. The Gangetic Plains

E. The Central Himalayas

F. The West Coast or Malabar

G. The Deccan Plateau

H. The Assam Zone

I. The Islands

A. The Western Himalayas

There are many high mountains in this region containing many important vegetation of the world. The region is spreaded over from Uttranchal in east to Kashmir in west. The average rainfall ranging from 100 to 200 centimetres. The climate changes are observed lower to higher regions from hot to cold as a result of which different type of vegetation are found in the region. The region has been sub-divided into three zones.

(i) The Basal Zone—It is also known as the outer hills or sub mountain zone. This zone lies at a height in between 300-1500 meters and damp and mostly sesamum, saal, Jamun trees are found where as babool, kamala, kauranda, trees or pulpy thuar, etc. in dry places and the pine trees at a height of 1000 meter or more are found. The soil vegetation is hardly grow in this area.

(ii) The Temperate Zone—This zone lies at a height in between 1500-3000 meters with moderate temperature. The rainfall and temperature are less as compared to the basal zone and snowfall occurs in winter. The sub-mountain areas have much vegetation and deciduous spear headed tress. The different varieties of trees like pine, deodar, oak, etc. are found depending upon the height. The white rose, barbari, pomegranate, from the class of brier vegetation are also found. Rice, saffron, walnut almond, apple, etc. are cultivated in the humid atmosphere of Kashmir.

(iii) Alpine Zone—The Zone above the height of 3500 meter is alpine zone and the area between the height 4500-5000 meters in designated as snowfield. The small tress and brushwoods are found in the alpine zone. The herbivorous vegetation is mostly found in snowfield area. The height of 3500 meters is known as "Timber line" because 4000-5000 metres containing sub-alpine and alpine grass grows at different height.

B. The Eastern Himalayas

This zone covers the area from Sikkim to upper Assam. The snow line at the zone is at the height not 5,500 meters higher than the western Himalayas zone. The temperature and rainfall are much more than the previous zone. The zone is sub-divided into three zones.

(a) Tropical sub-montane zone—The area above 1800 meters height having following vegetation.

(i) ***Sal Forests***—It includes Sal and savanna area containing saccharumant nairaza grass.

(ii) ***Riverain Forests***—The area contains mostly sesamum, catechum etc. trees.

(iii) ***Mixed Deciduous Forests***—contains arjuna, semal, kadamb, etc...

(iv) ***Moist Savana Forests*** —The grasses of different types are found in this area our of which Saccharum grass is most abundant.

(v) ***Ever Green Forests***—The area is always remain ever green with varieties of flora-fauna and spices.

(b) Temperate Zone—The area from 1800 meters to 3800 meters height is called as temperate zone having two types of vegetation.

(i) The lower part of the area contains trees having broad leaves like maple etc.

(ii) The upper part—which is cold contains spear headed trees like draw willow etc.

C. The Indus Plains of Western Deserts

The north western and plains are included in this zone. The geographical region consists of Great Rann of Kutch, Western Rajasthan, North Gujrat and Haryana plains. The temperature in this region remains high enough whereas the rainfall is scantly and less, as such spear headed trees are found in the forest of this area, however dense and sub-tropical forests are found in North Punjab and South Rajasthan because of humidity. The western part of Rajasthan with rainfall less than 20 centimetres has been desertified where erophytic vegetation like babool (Acacia nilotica), capparies deciduas, calotrops procera, desmostachya bipinnat, etc. are found.

D. The Gangetic Plains

Uttar Pradesh, Bihar, Bengal and a part of Orissa constitute the Gangetic region. The rainfall varies from 70 to 150 centimetres. The soil contains both clay and sand as such all types of vegetation is found in this region. The tropical forests exist in Uttar Pradesh and Orissa whereas dense forests are found in Bengal and Bihar. The mangrove vegetation like Raizoforia, Akathens, Abecenia, Soneracia, etc, are fond in the delta of Ganga-Brahamputra and sea-shore region. The sesamum, Acacia Nilotica, Capparis Decidua etc. in Uttar Pradesh plains whereas Butea Monosperma, Diospyros Melanoxylon. Arjuna, Adhatoda vasica, etc., are found in east Uttar Pradesh along the side of Vindhyachal hill areas. Clorkenna, Mauritania, etc. the bush covered vegetation is also found in this region.

E. The Central Himalayas

The area in between the Gangetic plain and Deccan plateau which includes Madhya Pradesh, Orissa, a part of North Gujarat is designated as the Central Himalayan Zone. The moderate temperature and excess rains are the characteristics of the area which is divided into three categories on the basis of vegetation:-

(i) Sal Forests—Madhya Pradesh, Chattisgarh and the eastern part of Orissa where the sal forests are found

(ii) Mixed Deciduous Forests—Madhya Pradesh and central part of Chattisgarh is covered by these forests where Sagwan, Arjuna, Dhak, Mangoes, Amaltash, etc. trees are present in large quantities.

(iii) Thorn Forests—The dry areas of Madhya Pradesh where thorny vegetation like babool, khejari, khair, etc. are present in large quantities.

F. The West Coast or Malabar

The biogeographical region between Western Ghat and West Coast which includes Southern Gujarat and extreme

South upper Kanyakumari is called as Malabar zone having plenty of rains. There are four types of forests found in this zone

(i) ***Tropical Moist-Evergreen or Rain forests***— These forests are mostly found at the down side of western Ghat nearby seaside. There are many variation and large number of trees with an average height of about 200 feet. The principal varieties are Gurjan, Hopia, Calophilim, Tactona, Adina, etc.

(ii) ***Mixed Deciduous or Monsoon forests***—The region of Western Ghat at a height of about 5000 feet is a place of monsoon forests. The forests are not dense and contains mostly sesamum, sagvan, bamboo, etc.

(iii) ***Temperate Forest***—These forests are situated on the Nilgiri has at a height upto 5000 feet. The forests are evergreen having sesamum, mukella, cardoernia, gordonia, etc. trees.

(iv) ***Mangrove Forests***—The costal areas of Mumbai and Kerala consist of mangrove forests having bush covered vegetation.

G. The Deccan Plateau

The south of Godavari river and South Peninsula except the western coast consisting of Andhra Pradesh, Tamilnadu and Karnataka is the deccan plateau region which is almost dry with stony table-land plateau and divided into two parts

(i) *Southern Plateau*—The average rainfall is about 100 centimetres and mostly tropical forests are found which contains sandalwood, salar, khejari, etc. trees.

(ii) *The Coromandal Coast*—The area except the southern plateau is known as Coromandal cost. The tropical evergreen forests are found in this region.

H. The Assam Zone

The north eastern part of India constitutes Assam zone. There is high degree of humidity and excess all rains in this area resulting evergreen forests of spear headed and all land is full of vegetation. The numerous kinds of vegetation in large quantities are found in these forests.

I. The Islands

Islands situated in the Bay of Bengal and Arabian sea from a group of this region. The vegetation is as the kind found in Malaysia and neighbouring countries. The vegetation is of the kind beach, evergreen mangroves and leafy one depending on the situation of the area.

Biodiversity

India is full of biodiversity having all the natural resources required for all kinds of living organisms. The area of the country is approximately 3.3 million square kilometres with a total population around one billion. The costal area is about 7,616 kilometres and total length of rivers is about 28,000 kilometres. There are 14 geographical regions of forests containing about 13,000 flowing vegetation, 20,000 funguses, 2000 insects, 2000 types of fishes, 1200 kinds of birds, 350 classes of mammals and 410 community of reptiles. 30 **"National parks"** scattered in different parts of the country covering one percent area and many **"Sanctuaries"** covering about 3.5 percent area of the total land area for the conservation of vegetable and animal kingdom of the country have been kept reserved. The conservation of biodiversity is quite essential to meet the requirement of growing population and necessary steps are being taken from local, national and international platforms to save the future generation.

The biodiversity of India is quite peculiar and highly categorized, 33 percent of vegetation belong to particular region and these are found mostly in North East, Western

Ghat, North-Western Himalayas and Andaman and Nicobar Islands. 49,219 out of 5,150 vegetation are regional and they belong 141 genera and 141 families. The Himalayas range contains about 3,500 whereas 1,650 vegetation category are found in Western Ghat. Similarly 62 percent roaming animals of particular cult are mostly concentrated at the Western Ghat region, so much so 50 percent lizards are regional and found mostly in Western Ghat area.

India is also a land of seasonal vegetation and there are as many as 167 kinds of seasonal and 320 forest based vegetation.

The Himalayas forests belong to temperate zone which are situated at north of Tropic of Cancer at a height in between 1780-3500 feet from sea level. The Eastern Himalayas has a different topography as such biodiversity of vegetation is very much regional. There are 60 percent regional vegetation in Sikkim only. The Eastern Himalayas has very rare vegetation like sapria himaliyana which has been noticed only two times since 1836. The Primitive Angiosperms like aluns, betular, magnolia, tetrocentron, etc. are also mainly found in this region.

In Western Ghat region about 1,600 out of 49,215 regional vegetations are distributed with in an area of 17,000 square kilometres.

Endangered and Endemic Species

The man has been able to take major risks in modifying local ecosystem to enhance the yield of a desired commodity but with the rise of civilization and modern technology, he cannot afford major risks in dealing with the functioning of the biosphere without understanding the environmental limitation of the local ecosystem.

Man, being an active agent of environmental changes, modified the ecosystem, exploited the natural resources and reduced the ecological diversity and complexity of the ecosystem and climax vegetation have been destroyed by human activities like deforestation and mass felling of trees, introduction of new types of vegetation at a place which were not previously present (Forests of Agriculture use). Man has introduced species of plants and animal into the areas beyond their native places, changed the farming practices to commercial products, used pesticides and herbicides to destroy weeds and bushes. Due to all these human activities many living organisms and already disappeared in the past, many are reducing fast and have reached to the point of extinction. The species, which are at the verge of disappearance, are called as "Endangered or Threatened" living beings. The International Union for Conservation of Natural Resource has published a "Red Book" showing a list of endangered species of vegetation and animals, which need conservation.

Endangered Vegetation

A large area of many forests are changing into denuded forests every year due to human activities resulting disappearance of several vegetation. There are about 15,000 vegetation are on the brink of disappearance and about 40,000 need immediate conservation otherwise disappear by the middle of next century. A list of 450 endangered vegetation species have been prepared by Botanical Survey of India which are at the verge of extinction a few of them are—

(i) Aconitum Deinorrihizum

(ii) Adansonia Digitata

(iii) Aradiostegsa Psendocystoperis

(iv) Asplenium Pumilum varhymenophylloids

(v) Atropa Acuminata

(vi) Botrychium Virginianum

(vii) Colchicum luteum

(viii) Commiphora Wightii
(ix) Diclipetra abuensis
(x) Isotes Retainlata
(xi) Marsilea Aegypticia
(xii) Ophiglossum Grimineun
(xiii) Rauvolfia Serpentina
(xiv) Rosa Involucrata
(xv) Santalum Album
(xvi) Selaginella Rajasthnensis

Endemic Plants

The plant areas generally are large because of good number of agencies are responsible for dissemination and magnification of the plant kingdom. Anyhow, there are a few plants which are found only in limited areas and are called as 'Endemic'. A stunning example is non-recurrent 'Metacilkoya' which is only available at a China Valley and red wood tree "Seekoya Samperyaries" found only at the sea shore valley of California.

India because of its typical position has all kinds of climatic conditions of the world as such all types of plants are found and many have been originated from India. There are about 21,000 kinds of non-endemic blossoming plants and 600 teridophyotiess in India. About 1000 plants which are endemic found in Himalayan region and 500 in southern India. The plants like

(i) Calotropis Jaiygantia
(ii) Diasoparrious Abeniun
(iii) Ferronia Lymana, etc.

(iv) Phykus Elastica

(v) Vitex Negundu

are a few kinds of endemic plants found in India.

Conservation of Plant Kingdom

The man has exploited the vegetation from the early days and experienced ill effects due to destruction of plants. The biotic component of which the plant is a part is quit essential to human being for his living and development. It is therefore, quite important to conserve the natural vegetation for the existence of man on the surface of earth.

The Indian culture, custom and tradition are mostly linked through region. It is because of saints the learned people of society at that time thought to give religious touch to all human activities in order to save the natural resources of the biosphere. The following examples are described for illustration—

(i) Do not disturb the plants after dusk as they sleep and take rest.

(ii) To have holy plant 'Basil' (Tulsi) in the courtyard and worship by offering water daily in morning and evening. It has a medicinal value and purify the atmosphere of house.

(iii) Do not inflict injury to plants because "Ten wells are equal to one broad well which in turn equal to one tank. Ten tanks are equal to one son and ten sons are equal to one tree".

(iv) Many trees have been recognized as a place of residence of God as give below.

Table 1

Trees and Residing Deities

S. No.	*Name of Tree*	*Name of Deity*
1	Ashok	Indra
2	Banyan (Bargad)	Brahma and Kuber
3	Kadamb	Lord Krishna
4	Camphor	Moon
5	Emblic Myrobalan (Amla)	Laxmi
6	Glomerata (Goolar)	Vishnu, Rudra
7	Melanoxylon (Tendu)	Gandhrva
8	Peepal	Vishnu, Laxmi, Paternal deity
9	Wood Apple (Bel-Patra)	Lord Shiva

The most stunning example is the sacrifice given by about 350 people before 270 years to save the green Khejari plants in the village Kejharli of Jodhpur under the leadership of a great women Amrata Devi; Amrata Devi belief was "Head cut, tree saved yet it is very cheap".

The world conservation strategy has made few recommendation to check, control and to make available the natural resources forever without effecting their quality, the recommendations are—

(1) Constitutional provision for the protection of Natural Resources.

(2) Special legislation of Act to achieve the object of conservation.

(3) Involvement of people for the implementation of policies.

(4) Awareness amongst the people in framing and implementation of the rules.

(5) Special attention by the administration for the implementation of rules framed.

(6) Timely analysis of the rules and amendment accordingly.

There are two methods adopted for plant conservation.

(i) In Situ conservation—The 'Reserve Areas' have been declared as many parts of country for the conservation of living organisms in natural environments in Situ process of conservation.

(ii) Ex-Situ conservation—In this method the plants are shifted from their areas and are conserved in artificially made areas which are known as 'Hereditary Centres' and 'Flora Garden' where seeds pollen, seed-leaf, eggs etc. of the living organisms facing extinction and useful are stored in the reproduction banks from which new products are produced and established in flora garden or natural habitat.

Endangered Animals

The human activities have led to the extinction of many animal species, the giant animals are more susceptible and face extinction as "Flighltless Docta Bird" of Malaysia 'Rhinoceros' of Java, "Lion and Tiger" of India. The situation with respect to these animals is very critical and hopeless and require immediate measures for their conservation.

The list of endangered animals shows that 25 percent animals of the world are facing extinction. The Zoological Survey of India has prepared a list according to which 81 mammals, 38 birds, 18 reptiles and a few roaming animals are in difficult position and a few might disappear for ever if protective measures are not taken. The endangered animals in India are:

(i) Dolphin

(ii) Flying Squirrel

(iii) Great Indian Bustard

(iv) Himalayan Brown Bear

(v) Hyaena

(vi) Indian Wild Ass.

(vii) Leopard

(viii) Lion Tailed Macaque

(ix) Python

(x) Rhinoceros

(xi) Siberian White Crane

(xii) Tiger

(xiii) Whale

In olden times the man used to fight with the giant wild animals to prove his valour, which changed in due course of time as fashion and status symbol. The Royal families used to have their own hunting grounds where commoners were not allowed to go for hunt. The scenario has completely changed under the British rule. The military personnel, civil servants and tea garden owners had started hunting for the sake of entertainment and to from image amongst the local people as the hunting was recognized as a honourable practice by highly placed people. The figure of killings of wild animals are surprisingly enough to reveal that one British Officer killed 50 tiger in 21 days; one British Railway Officer killed about 100 tigers in the span of four years (1850-54). In Bengal one tea gardener killed almost 100 rhinoceros. In Kashmir one British hunter killed 58,613 wild ducks. A King killed 616 tigers while another king 1100 tigers in their lifetime. So much so in one of the hunting programme held at Cooch Behar the number of wild animals hunted are most fascinating; 370 tigers, 208 rhinoceros, 430 wild buffaloes and 324 stags. Much of the wildlife is peculiar in the sub-continent and not found anywhere else in the world are

(i) Black buck

(ii) Four horned Antelope

(iii) Indian Lion

(iv) Kashmir Stag

(v) Nilgai

(vi) One horned Rhinoceros

(vii) Spotted Chital, the most beautiful amongst all dears

(viii) Swamp Dear

(ix) Wild Ox

Wildlife Conservation

For the conservation of endangered animals, Government of India has undertaken special projects which have been implemented successfully in collaboration with the state Government. A few are listed below—

(i) Gir Lion Project —The project was started by government of Gujarat in 1972 to cheek the abatement and breeding of Pantheralion persica (Asian tiger)

(ii) Tiger Project—The tiger reserves areas have been made in the various parts of the country to save tigers from extinction. The various states have started the tiger projects in 1970.

(iii) Crocodile Breeding and Management Project—To conserve and increase in number, the crocodile breeding and management projects have been undertaken and breeding centres have been opened in many states in 1975.

The other endangered species are also being protected in all the above projects.

National Parks and Sanctuaries

In order to provides natural habitat to wildlife and other living organisms to protect and develop in their own environment without human interference and activities several "Biosphere Reserves" have been built up in many parts of the country. The biosphere reserve includes "National Parks" and "Sanctuaries" which are looked after by the "Indian Board of Wildlife' and Act 1972 governs the conservation and protection of endangered species both inside and outside of the forest areas. Presently, the country has 86 national parks, 480 sanctuaries and 17 tiger reserves covering 4.5 percent of the total geographical area of the country. A "wild-life week" is also observed in the first week of October every year.

National Parks

The national parks have been established to conserve the objects of natural and historical importance and the natural environment. The ultimate aim has been to protect and conserve the living organisms in their natural habitat. There are two following zone of the national parks.

(i) Buffer Zone—The human and other activities are allowed to some extent in the buffer zone

(ii) Core Zone—Any kind of activities are prohibited in the core zone.

The boundaries of these areas vary from 40 to 3162 square kilometres which is announced under law.

These national parks conserve and protect many rare and endangered species. The first National Park was established in 1936 which is now known as "Jim Corbett Park" situated in Nainital, Uttranchal. This list of few National Parks is as under—

Table 2

Important National Parks

S. No.	*Name of Park*	*Place*	*State*
1	Bandhavgarh	Shahdol	Madhya Pradesh
2	Bandipur	Mysore	Karnataka
3	Borivili	Mumbai	Maharashtra
4	Corbett	Nainital	Uttranchal
5	Dudhwa	Lakhimpur Kheri	Uttar Pradesh
6	Eravikulan	Idduki	Kerala
7	Gir	Junagarh	Gujarat
8	Guindy	Chennai	Tamilnadu
9	Hazaribagh	Hazaribagh	Jharkhand
10	Kanha	Mandla	Madhya Pradesh
11	Kaziranga	Jorhat	Assam
12	Khongechandzenda	Gangtok	Sikkim
13	Nagerhole	Coorg	Karnataka
14	Nawegaon	Bhandra	Maharastra
15	Pench	Nagpur	Maharastra
16	Rohia	Kulu	Himachal Pradesh

17	Shivpur	Shivpuri	Madhya Pradesh
18	Todotra	Chandrapur	Maharastra
19	Valavadar	Bhavnagar	Gujarat

Sanctuaries—The concept of wildlife as a 'thing of beauty' and a gift of nature which need to be preserved, rather a 'game' to be hunted, developed soon after the independence. The former hunting ground have been converted to "Wildlife Sanctuaries' where all the wild animals and birds are to be fully protected so that they will not become extinct. Project tiger was also launched with the object of preserving and increasing tiger population by safeguarding the tiger, animals of its prey and its habitat in selected areas of the country. The areas of these sanctuaries vary from 61 to 7818 square kilometre depending upon the number of species present in the area. The list of a few sanctuaries is as follows—

Table 3

Important Sanctuaries

S.No.	*Name of Sanctuaries*	*Place*	*State*
1	Chandraprabha	Varanasi	Uttar Pradesh
2	Dachigam	Srinagar	Jammu & Kashmir
3	Ghana	Bharatpur	Rajasthan
4	Ghatprabha	Betgaum	Karnataka
5	Jaladapara	Jalpaiguri	West Bengal
6	Kutree	Bastar	Chattisgarh
7	Manas	Barpeta	Assam
8	Melapattu	Nellor	Andhra Pradesh

9	Mudumalai	Niligiris	Tamilnadu
10	Nal Sarovar	Ahmedabad	Gujarat
11	Palamu	Daltonganj	Jharkhand
12	Periyar	Idduki	Kerala
13	Ranganthittoo	Mysore	Karnataka
14	Ranthambor	Sawai Madhopur	Rajasthan
15	Similipal	Mayurbhanj	Orissa
16	Sultanpur	Gurgaon	Haryana
17	Sunderbans	24 Purganas	West Bengal
18	Sariska	Alwar	Rajasthan

Hot Spots

Hot Spots are those place on earth where the living organisms (animal and plant) are:

(i) Extremely rich in species

(ii) Possessing high endemism

(iii) Having a constant threat for the existence.

There are about 25 hot spots in the world and two such spots are situated in India and have extended to the neighbouring countries also. The first hot spot lies in the area of Western Ghat and the second in the Eastern Himalayas region. The flora wealth and endemism is observed in abundance in addition to reptiles, mammals, insects, etc.

The hot spots in India are quite far away from each other, yet there is distinct differentiation and similarity between the bio-organisms found in these places for example. The Western Ghats and Eastern Himalayas are rich in flora and fauna wealth and endemism, not only in flowering plants but also in reptiles, amphibian, shallow-tailed butter fillies, etc. There 2550 endemic plant species out of 4250 plants in Sikkim area and a total of 2000 species out of 5800 are endemic in India. The common flora species are—

(i) Cotoneaster Buxifolica

(ii) Fragrentissima

(iii) Gautheria

(iv) Hyper Hookerianum

(v) Japonica

(vi) Lamina

(vii) Lonicera Ligustrina

(viii) Rhododendron

(ix) Ternstromia

Amongst fauna, the following species are found—

(i) Fairy Blue Bird

(ii) Hawks

(iii) Himalayan Bear

(iv) Hornbull

(v) Lizard

(vi) Nilgai

(vii) Nilgiri Pinemarten

Natural Resources

The nature is kind enough and has gifted all the necessary resources in ample amount though not uniformly distributed all over the country.

Atmosphere and Climate

The atmosphere of the country is quite healthy and people by and large are happy and healthy. The problem of atmospheric pollution is mostly confined to metropolitan cities like Bombay, Chennai, Delhi, Kolkata and Urban cities which have been developed due to industrialization, the cities like Banglore, Bhilwara, Kanpur, Ludhiana, Patna, etc. The climatic conditions is so much contrast that the effect of pollutants is not visible to a large extent except a few sensitive areas where sufficient measures have been taken by the Government agencies.

India with its vast size and marked variations in terrain is a land of climate contrast. During summer temperature may occasionally shoot upto 55^{0}C in certain parts of Rajasthan and South West Punjab and in winter night, the temperature may go down as low as -50^{0}C. Similarly, Cherapunji, with its annual rainfall of 1084 centimetres, is the wettest place in the world, the dry regions of West Rajasthan get no more than 13 centimetres of annual rainfall. In between these extremities, there are regions of equable moderate uniform conditions.

The Tropic of Cancer divides India into two halves:

(i) Southern India which is a tropical zone

(ii) Northern India which is a sub-tropical zone

The most important factor in shaping India's climate condition is monsoon, that affect almost all parts of the country with varying intensity and duration. The important characteristic is the complete reversal of the winds which leads to the alternation of season. On the basis of monsoon variation the year is divided into four seasons which are—

Table 4

Seasons and Duration

S.No.	*Season*	*Duration*
1.	The cold weather	December–February
2.	The hot weather	March–May
3.	The South–West Monsoon (Rain)	June–September
4.	The Retreating South–West Monsoon (Rain)	October-November

Land Resources

India has a geographical area of about 329 meter hectares but statistical information is available only for about 305 meter hectares. About 50 percent land is under cultivation as compared to 11 percent of world's average. The forest areas are around 19.7 percent and 30.3 percent of area is being used as commercial, residential industrial, etc. activities. Taking into account the total land resources including hills, mountains, lakes, rivers and land of call descriptions, the availability of land per head in India comes to about 0.58 hectare and the percentage of arable land to the geographical area in India works out at 52.7 percent only.

(1) Soil Types

Soil quality is an important factor for agricultural activities. The soil provides necessary nourishment through the minerals and humidity percent. India with its vast land surface and divers relief features, possesses a large variety of soils, which, according to the National Council of Agriculture Research, are classified into the following eight categories.

Table 5

Soil Type, Characteristics and Existing Area

S.No.	Type	Characteristics/ cultivation	Area
1.	Alluvial soil	Sediments deposition by sea & rivers, Deficient in nitrogen and humus and need fertilizers. Suitable for cereals, pulse, sugarcane, oilseed, vegetable, etc.	The plains from Punjab to Assam, valleys of Narmada, Tapti, Mahanadi, Godavari, Krishna, Cuvery Rivers (M.P., Gujarat, A.P., T.N. etc.)
2.	Black Cottons Soil	Black, sticky and hard containing compounds of Iron and aluminium. Deficient in nitrogen, phosphates and organic matter but rich in potash, lime, aluminium, calcium and magnesium. Suitable for cotton, cereals, oil seeds, vegetables.	Madhya Pradesh, Gujarat, Karnataka, Andhra Pradesh and Tamilnadu.
3.	Red Soil	Crystalline and metamorphic rich in ferromagenese but deficient in nitrogen humid. Suitable for rice, tobacco, vegetables.	Southern Peninsula upto Jhansi in North, Kutch in West and Rajmahal Hills in East.
4.	Lateritic Soil	Rich in Iron oxide. Deficient in nitrogen, phosphorus, potash and magnesium,	Western Ghats, Rajmahal hills, hilly eastern region, Karnataka, A.P.,

	suitable for rice, ragi and sugarcane.	Kerala, Orissa and West Bengal.

(ii) Land Degradation

The land degradation is a world wide problem. The problem is mainly due to land slide, soil erosion and other factors but by for the most contributing factors are the human activities. The problem of land degradation in India is due to desertification and human activities mainly industrialization and urbanization.

(i) *Industrialization and Urbanization*—Under the pretext of development and civilization, the arable land has been encroached. The scenario of the area has been changed like a concrete jungle. The debris and junks have been dumped on the surface area resulting in land degradation.

(ii) *Dams and Canals have been constructed for the power requirement and irrigation*—A large amount of collected water has destroyed the inner land (bed-soil) of the area. Irrigation through canals in the initial stage has done miracles and many uncultivated areas have been brought under cultivation but later on it has been proved to be a curse because of water-logging problem in the area. The ground water has turned brackish and saline, The soil has become friable with the result that the dry farming of easier crops is not viable.

(iii) *The plantation of 'Eucalyptus' trees on large scale on free land*—resulting saline soil and lowering of water level of the area.

(iv) The mechanical farming has also contributed to the degradation of land which over-turns the land completely where as the traditional way of ploughing

simply shuffles the soil which keeps the soil quality intact.

(*v*) The blasting of mountains for rubble and mining activities for building materials have also changes the characteristics of the adjoining land of the area.

(*vi*) *Desertification*—The Thar Desert or the great Indian desert with an area of about 3,20,000 square kilometre (12% of geographical area of India) lies at the north west of the Malawa Plateau.

The desert, which is made up of sand, interrupted by rocky hills and waterless valleys, begins from the western Arawali regions and spreaded on the following parts of the country.

Desert Area and Regions

S. No.	*State*	*Percent*
1	Rajasthan	62
2	Gujarat	19
3	Punjab and Haryana	09
4	Andhra Pradesh and Karnataka	10

Division of Thar Desert

The Arawali Hills about 692 kilometres long divides the Thar Desert in two parts.

a. Arid Sandy Plain—The desert area west and north-west of Aravalli terrain in the Thar desert which includes 11 Districts of Rajasthan viz., Barmer, Bikaner, Churu, Jaisalmer, Jalore, Jhunjhunu, Jodhpur, Pali, Nagaur, Sikar, Sriganganagar.

b. Semi Desert Plain—It is a contagious area spreaded over the south–east of Aravalli Mountain. It is a semi-desert which includes 16 districts of Rajasthan which are

Ajmer, Alwar, Banswara, Baran, Bhartpur, Bhilwara, Bundi, Chittorgarh, Dholpur, Dungarpur, Jaipur, Jhalawar, Kota, Tonk, Sawaimadhopur, Sirohi.

The Thar desert is progressing towards western Uttar Pradesh and Delhi due to storm and high speed wind. The fertile land in the neighbouring states and ecosystem of the area are being affected. The natural vegetarian area is reducing day by day which has resulted in the formation of sand-dunes and dried atmosphere. The dust-storm lead to sand deposition in the bed of rivers and lakes resulting shallowness of rivers and lakes.

The land of neighbouring states Punjab, Haryana, Uttar pradesh, Delhi, Gujrat etc. will become infertile in due course of time if the propagation of desert is not checked in time, it has been concluded that the Thar desert is spreading north-south ward at a rate of one and half kilometres per year. The reasons attributed for desert spreading are :

1. Sweeping of sand
2. Climate change
3. Excessive grazing
4. Deforestation

Climate of Thar Desert

The principal climatic symptom of desert are

i. Stormy hot air (135 km/hr. or above).
ii. Low relative humidity.
iii. Temperature variation (Very high in day time and pleasant in night).
iv. Seasonal Temperature (0-25^{0}C in winter, 25-55^{0}C in summer).
v. Extreme drought

vi. More evaporation and less rain.

vii. Scanty rainfall. (10 centimetres)

viii. Soil – Saline, Marl, light texture, low water holding capacity.

ix. Sand dunes. (58 percent of total area)

The Central Arid Zone Research Institute has been established in 1957 at Jodhpur to look into the problem of desertification. The object assigned is to check the spreading of desert and convert the area into grass land. The latest report suggests that the spreading of desert area has been controlled to some extent but the environmental deterioration of the surrounding areas of the desert is still taking place.

Plantation of Trees to Check Expansion of Desert

It has been found that the following types of trees are helpful in checking the progress of desert:

i. Acacia Nilotica. (Local Babool)

ii. Acacia Senegal. (Kumta)

iii. Acacia Tortilrs. (Israreli Babool)

iv. Ailanthus Excelsa (Aradoo)

v. Albizia Lebbeck. (Siras)

vi. Azadiraachta Indica. (Neem)

vii. Balanites Roxburghii. (Hingota)

viii. Copparis Decidua. (Kair)

ix. Cordia Dichotoma (Lasoraha, Gaunda)

x. Prosopis Cinerana (Khejari)

xi. Prosopis jubflora. (English Babool)

xii. Tecomella Undulata (Rohiraha)

xiii. Ziziphus Nummularia. (Beri)

The Central Arid Zone Research Institute has formulated a programme of air spraying the seed of lasiurus hirsutus (Sevan Grass) in order to cover the soil with grass which is very much liked by the animals. A great part of the Thar Desert has been declared as "Thar Desert Biosphere Reserve" through the wildlife protection Act 1972 where the vegetation and animals are conserved.

It has been proved that there were different kinds of land structure at the places where deserts exist now. The most interesting example is the Thar-desert of India. It has been established beyond doubt that the rivers like Saraswati and others were flowing in the area as covers of peral and shell have been found on excavation. There was a well developed civilization which could be ascertained by looking the remains of Kalibanga and Rangmahal.

The desertification is a natural process but it is a sequential process brought about by the natural factors like water, air, land or vegetation and animals together with man as a result of which desertification process takes place. The natural process is rather slow and take a pretty long time so that the ecosystem acquire adaptability. The human interference makes the process fast as such there is a great distortion of ecosystem in very short period resulting disappearance of many species. Keeping this in mind the desert management programme should be framed to check expansion of desert rather than to convert desert areas into green areas which may or rather would lead to a different kind of disturbance in ecosystem resulting another type of disorderness. The nature has created everything in a proportionate order to keep the balance in the biosphere in which living organisms can exist.

Forest Resources

Amongst the most valuable resources of India, the forests play a magnificent role in enhancing the quality environment. The total forest cover which includes dense forest, open forest and mangroves forest is estimated to be 6773 million heactares, which is about 19.39 percent of country's geographical area as compared to 33 percent in other countries. The distribution is as follows.

Forest Degradation

In the beginning of human civilization and developmental activities, there was 60 percent forest of the total geographical area of the world which has been reduced to 40 percent by the year 1850. At present, it is only 26 percent. There was about 74.8 million hectare forest in India at the time of independence which is now around 67.73 million hectares. The total forest area is as under – (100 hectare = 1 square kilometre)

Forest Area and Type

S. No.	*Type of Forest*	*Area (Million hectares)*
1	Spear headed	4.2
2	Shorea Robusta (Saal)	11.6
3	Tectora Grandis (Sagvan)	8.9
4	Mixed Vegetation	43.03
	Total	67.73

The degradation of forests has occurred due to deforestation on account of

i. Felling of trees for the wood.

ii. Grazing in excess of carrying capacity.

iii. Encroachment for other purposes like agricultural, urban settlements, Industrialization etc.

iv. Shifting of cultivation area.

v. Illicit felling and theft for timber.

vi. Diversion for no-forest purposes like mining, dames construction of highways, etc. It has been estimated that the forest cover of the Eastern Himalayan region has been reduced to 1,10,000 square kilometres from 3,40,000 square kilometers, which contains only 53,000 square kilometers as dense forests. The another survey reveals that the forest cover of the country's is decreasing at a rate of 1.5 crore hectares every year and if it is allowed to continue, there will be no sign of forests, in the country.

As per standard norms of ecological aspects, the forest cover should be approximately 33 percent of the total geographical area that is only 20 percent at present.

Conservation

The national forest policy aims at keeping one-third of the total geographical area under forests, but due to pressure in population and consequent heavy pressure on the forest land for different socio-economic purposes, forest area has been lost during past half century. The production forestry envisages raising of industrial plantation on large scale to meet the industrial raw materials, social forestry programme, on the other hand confined to the uncultivated lands and also the farm lands. It is for wood-based production system for site and habitat improvement together with major and minor forest products. Three different schemes have been launched.

(i) Mixed plantation on waste land.

(ii) Reafforestation of degraded forests and raising shelter belts.

(iii) Rural flu-wood plantation for the supply of flue-wood and fodder.

Conclusion

The evergreen forests of Mt. Abu are depleting fast because of illicit felling of trees and the area is being deprived of vegetation. The harmful plants like Lantana, Carrot-grass have been grown up instead. These plants ooze out vapours of poisonous chemicals (Pheromones) which does not allow any vegetation in the area. Immediate action should be taken for the conservation and renewal of vegetation of Mt. Abu, the only hill station of Rajasthan.

Water Resources

The water is one of the most important natural resource and plays an important role in the biosphere. It is quite abundant as such it is extravagantly wasteful, misused and has been grossly underpriced and often supplied completely free. It is generally believed that water consumption grows with the income and population. The extravagant domestic consumption has contributed to the shortage of water in many parts of the country.

Though water is quite abundant in nature, only one percent of the total world water is available for all human activities. Water is literally vital, without it life would not exist and even one percent of water source is enough for all, as water is infinitely renewable. In March 2003 in Kyoto, Japan, world water conference was held and the year 2003 had been declared as the international year of 'Fresh Water' and the Earth Summit at Johannesburg, South Africa held in 2002 agreed to enhance the number of people with safe access to clear water and basic sanitation double fold by 2015.

Water Scenario of India

The problem of water in India is quite peculiar as there are some parts having enough water, many with insufficient and a few with no water. The people by and large were sensitive enough to conserve the sources and use of water. In the modern period of civilization the water is now distributed through pipelines, the people have become careless and forgotten the technique of conservation which has created the problem in urban areas and even in cities situated by the side of rivers. There are cities where water is supplied twice in a week for few hours and the people by and large have not taken any interest to revive the neglected sources of water which has been converted into dumping places of domestic and other wastes. The problem of water has again become complicated because of industrialization where natural water is consumed and polluted water is discharged into the main streams. The problem is again aggravated by the use of synthetic manures, faming commercial crops and continuation of agricultural production through out the year which demand more water.

Utilization of Water

The water is used almost in every walk of life and human activities. Man needs water all the time in all the activities except breathing and sleeping. The utilization of water in India can be studied under the following head

(a) Direct use—Man requires water for drinking, cooking bathing, gardening, cleaning, etc. (100-200 litres a day).

(b) Industrial use—The industrial requirement of water is very large and there are as many industries as water resources.

India was overwhelmingly an agricultural country before independence, lagging behind the desired level of industrialization. The country is now, more or less self sufficient in the production of consumer goods. The major industries manufacturing different products and providing employment to people next to agriculture sector are—

Table 11

Major Industries of India

S. No.	Industry	Location
1.	Aluminium	Alupuram, Alwaye, Belgaum, Hirakud Jayakaynagar, Koraput, Korba, Mettur and Ratangiri
2.	Automobiles	Chennai, Faridabad, Gurgaon, Kolkata, Ludhiana, Mumbai, Mysore, Pune, Tirupati.
3.	Cement	Andhra Pradesh, Bihar, Chhatisgarh, Gujarat, Jharkhand, Karnataka, Madhya Pradesh, Rajasthan, Tamilnadu.
4.	Cotton and textile	Andhra Pradesh, Gujarat, Karnataka, Maharashtra, Rajasthan, Uttar Pradesh, Tamilnadu.
5.	Fertilizers	Baroda, Cochin, Durgapur, Gorakhpur, Kanpur, Kota, Namrup, Nangal, Neyveli, Rourkela, Sindri, Trombay, Varanasi, Visakhapatnam.
6.	Heavy Electrical and Machinery	Bhopal, Durgapur, Hardwar, Hyderabad, Ranchi, Visakhapattnam, Tiruchirapalli,

7.	Paper and Paper Board	Andhra Pradesh, Bengal, Bihar, Chhatisgarh, Jharkhand, Karnataka, Madhya Pradesh, Tamilnadu.
8.	Sugar	Andhra Pradesh, Bihar, Jharkhand, Karnataka, Maharastra, Uttar Pradesh, Tamilnadu.

Apart from above, there are many more industries like leather goods, railways, shipbuilding, tractors, etc. are operating in many parts of the country. The small scale and cottage industries estimated to above 3370 lakhs producing many products are also working. In Rajasthan, there are many small and large units of textile industries at Barmer, Bhilwara, Kishnagarh, Pali and Sanganer which consumes a large quantity of water. The Copper and Zinc plants are situated at Khetri, Chittorgarh, Debari, Udaipur. There are many cement plants at Beawar, Chittorgarh, Lakheri, Morak, Nimbahera, etc. Many leather tanneries are working nearby Tonk region. The industrial town Kota which has been known as Kanpur of Rajasthan has many industrial complexes.

(c) Water for Agriculture—Agriculture is the backbone of country's economy, which provides employment to approximately 64 percent working people. There are three major crop seasons viz. Kharif, Rabi, and Zaid. The areas which are extensively irrigated, grow three to four crops pre year. Agricultural crops can be broadly divided into four categories, viz.

(i) Food Crops—It consists of cereals (Bajra, Jowar, Wheat, Rice, Maize etc., and pulses Arhar, Gram. Masur, Moong etc.

(ii) Non food crops—These are cash crops like Cotton, Jute, Sugarcane, Tobacco, etc.

(iii) Horticulture Crops—Fruit, Vegetables, Coconut, Cashew, etc.

Irrigation Facilities

Water is very important for the survival of all forms of life plant and animal kingdom. The country by virtue of it peculiar characteristics with the Aravalis, Himalayas, Satpura, Vindhyachal areas and the Deccan plateau running through it has vast water resources which have not been tapped and using only recognized means of irrigation like wells, tubewells, tanks and canals. The all seasons rivers and canals are most important means of irrigation.

The total area of country is 32.8 million hectares out of which 16.2 million hectares is under cultivation. The Irrigation facilities is only available on 4.5 million hectares land while total irrigated land is approximately 8 million hectares and rest 8.2 million hectares land is cultivated during the rainy season.

Water for Hydroelectric Power

The hydroelectric power is generated by constructing dams on principal rivers. Table 12 includes a few dams where hydroelectric power is generated. The table below lists dams exclusively used for power generation.

Table 12

Hydroelectric Power Projects

S.No.	*Name*	*Place*	*Capacity*
1	Damodar Valley	Bokaro, Durgapur, Chandarpur	1077 and 104 Mega Watt 5.51 lakh hectares land Irrigated
2	Bhakra Nangal	Gangalwal Kotwal	1204 Mega Watt 14.6 lakh hectares land Irrigated

3	Chambal	Gandhisagar Ranapratapsagar Kota Dam	3.86 Mega Watt 5.15 Lakh hectares land irrigated
4	Hirakund	Hirakund	37.500 K.W.
5	Gandak	Talwara	15 Mega Watt 11.98 Lakh hectares land Irrigated
6	Mahi	Banswara	40,000 K.W. 2.75 lakh hectares land Irrigated
7	Matatila	Jhansi	10,000 K.W.
8	Mayurakshi	Mushirdabad	4,000 K.W. 2.91 lakh hectares land Irrigated
9	Tungbhadra	Mallupuram	72,000 K.W. 4.97 Lakh hectares land Irrigated

Growing Water Scarcity

Though water is quite abundant in nature, still surpassingly, it is a scare commodity because

(i) Water is not uniformly distributed throughout the surface of the earth.

(ii) Water has many important application as an engineering material.

(iii) Primary water source is rainfall which has been affected by the human activities.

(iv) Secondary sources of water (surface and underground water) have been polluted.

(v) Growing population, urbanization and industrialization—In earlier days, the water has been mostly used for domestic, agriculture and a few miscellaneous works. The people are mostly dependent on rain and natural water resources of the area. The people had developed habit to do maximum work till the last drop of water. The water was not wasted and conserved in order to meet any water shortage problem.

In the modern age of civilization, the technology has provided many such things which could not have been imagined by the older generation and which has made life so comfortable that by and large people have becomes carefree and irresponsible to some extent. This tendency has developed extravagant use of water by the people as it has been grossly underpriced and supplied more or less free at the door.

It is generally believed that water consumption grows with the population. The availability of water was 5326 cubic litres per person per year in 1947 which has been reduced to 2267 cubic litres in 1991. The demand of water in all areas was 550 cubic litres which has increased 750 cubic litre and it would be 1050 cubic litres by 2025. The water which is received in the form of rainfall and ice is approximately 4000 cubic metres. The most of rain water flows over and only 1670 cubic litres water is collected in various rivers, tanks, wells, etc. Out of which only 690 cubic litres is used for different purpose by the people. The shortage of water is therefore felt because of improper use of water in different sector.

The change of irrigation way of leather-bucket bullock system to motor pump system has also led excessive use resulting shortage of water. Similarly the leakages in pipe lines of public distribution system and open hydrant also add to the problem of water scarcity. The immense demand of various industries for good quality of water has increased the water requirement considerably and the worst part of industrial activities that most of the industrial effluents have polluted the water resources and that polluted water present in the area is as of no water in the area.

These above discussed factors along with many other, the problem of water shortage has reached to danger level.

During the last five year span the rate of discharge of underground water has increased by 10 percent over the recharging rate. If this process continues in the same way, it is feared that the underground water storage would be finished by 2010. It has been therefore suggested the water resources of the country be declared as a 'National Sources'. In this context, the Government of India has constituted a body to find solution of linking all the major rivers of north, east, south and west in order to achieve uniform distribution or water and to control flood and drought. This might lead to disturbances in the ecosystem which should also be kept in mind before implementation otherwise the future generation will suffer a lot and curse their old generation who had created the problem for their own benefit. Here it should be mentioned that the traditional ways of conservation of water and neglected old resources should be looked into. 'The Watershed Management Programme' is working on these lines and a combination of old traditional way and modern technological methods of water conservation have been worked out which is effective in solving the problem of water shortage to a great extent.

Food Resources

The terrestrial agriculture, has been a principal source of food for human beings, yet it is not sufficient in the present day context of growing population. The different agriculture products require different typed of climatic condition and land structure as such no nation is self sufficient for all types of agriculture products. In a nation itself all kinds of agriculture commodity cannot be produced at one place for example. Bengal, Bihar and Orissa are rice producing states whereas Uttar Pradesh is known for wheat, sugarcane, Gujrat for groundnut, cotton, and pulses and Rajasthan for millet, maize, jowar, pearlmillet.

Green Revolution

The agriculture activities are totally dependent on the rain at the time of independence. There was a great shortage of cereals and pulses as such the public distribution system through rationing introduced. The growing population has also intricated the problem. Surprisingly, agriculture is the backbone of the country's economy, which provides direct employment to about 64 per cent of working people, contributes about 26 per cent of gross domestic products and earns about 18 per cent of total export income. Besides, it provides a vast market of industrial products as such the agriculture sector should be accorded a pride place which was not done till the "Green Revolution" programme has been initiated as a result of which, India not only came out of pauperism but exporting many agricultural products. The following table incorporation data of food crops before and after the green revolution.

Table 18

Production of Crops Before and After Green Revolution

S.No.	*Crops*	*Production Kg/hectare* *Before*	*After*
1	Cotton	88	213
2	Food grains	522	1,551
3	Maize	547	1,721
4	Oil seeds	481	840
5	Rice	668	1,895
6	Sugarcane	33,000	70,000
7	Wheat	663	2,470

The use of land in the country for agriculture commodity is as shown in following table—

Table 19

Present Land use in India

1	Geographical Area	328.73 million hectares
2	Net Cultivated Area	136.18 million hectares
3	Net Irrigated Area	43.05 million hectares
4	Rainfed Area	93.12 million hectares
5	Percentage Irrigated Area	68.47 million hectares
6	Percentage Rainfed Area	60.40 million hectares

Major Crops and Seasons

There are three major crop seasons in India, viz.

(i) **Kharif Crops**—The Kharif crops are cotton, jowar, jute, maize, ragi and sugarcane which are also known as monsoon crops and are sown in the months of June and July and are harvested in autumn (September and October).

(ii) **Rabi Crops**—They are sown in between October and December and harvested in April and May. Crops like barley, linseed, mustard, peas, pulses, and rapeseed are 'Rabi Crops'.

(iii) **Zaid** in the summer season—groundnut, maize, rice, sun flower, vegetables are 'Zaid Crops'.

The areas, which are extensively irrigated, the farmers grow four crops per year. The Indian farmers are very hard working, round the year, day and night, they toil, deprived off many worldly charms. They contribute too much towards the economy of the country, yet their contribution is not recognized, and are looked as downcast community of the human society. The pity of all above this they to not get even the actual cost of their products.

The agricultural crops can be broadly divided into four classes—

(i) **Food Crops**—They consist of cereals (bajra, jowar, maize, rice, wheat etc. and pulses (arhar, gram, masur, moong etc.)

(ii) **Non Food Crops**—There are number of cash crops like cotton, Jute, sugarcane, tobacco, etc. which are known as non-food crops.

(iii) **Plantation Crops**—Coffee, rubber, tea, etc. are included among the plantation crops.

(iv) **Horticulture Crops**—Cashew, coconut, fruits, vegetables etc. are the horticulture crops.

Effect of Green Revolution

(i) Food Grains—The situation on food front was quite comfortable with stock of 18.2 million tones against the normal requirement of 15.4 million tonnes, which is continuously increasing and at present it has swelled to over 60 million tonnes.

Although the food grain position has improved a lot but the condition of farmers has not improved, and also the agriculture land quality has been destroyed by the use of chemical fertilizer, pesticides, canal irrigation and mechanical process of farming. In addition, the area of arable land has also reduced because of urbanization and industrialization.

(ii) Use of Fertilizers, Insecticides and Pesticides—The chemical fertilizers have been recommend to make up the deficiency of nitrogen, phosphorous and potassium of the soil. The excessive use of fertilizers has polluted the soil and water. The use of fertilizers was practically nil in 1950-51 is now being used to the tune of 60 kg. per hectare. The fertilizers increase the food crops production initially but produce salinity on the soil surface and destroy properties of the land. In addition, the water is also polluted. (water with high nitrated concentration causes obstacle in the absorption capability of oxygen by the haemoglobin present in blood, which may lead to mental diseases and an anaemia).

The insecticides and pesticides no doubt kills the insects and pests but remain in the soil as they are not decomposed. The crops absorb these chemicals, which makes 'Food Chain' and the amount of these chemicals go on increasing. The process in known as 'Bio-magnification'. These chemicals are harmful to living organisms. The use of insecticides and pesticides has been banned in many countries but it is still in use in India.

The effect of insecticides like B.H.C., D.D.T., Aldrin and Linden remains for 30 to 45 days. Aldrin is widely used insecticides in India which is quite dangerous to animal life. There are about 10,000 chemicals which are produced in the past 40 years and no body knows the poisonous effect of about 80 percent of these chemicals. The use of these chemicals must be stopped and to solve the problem of food grain production and protection, the search of such chemicals which do not affect the soil and water should the made, till than use bio-manure be propagated.

(iii) Canal Irrigation and Mechanical Farming—The Irrigation facilities have been much improved during the green evolution. A wide network of canals has been expanded to many areas which has increased the production of food crops on the land but has created many adverse effects on the nearby and arable land. The environment is being damaged and the agriculture land is becoming infertile. The two important problems which are faced by the farmers are—

(a) Water Logging—The retention of water on a land for a considerable period is said to be water logging. The productivity and fertility of land is adversely affected. The National Commission of Agriculture (1976) has defined an area is water logged, "When the water-table rise to an extent that the soil pores in the root zone of a crop becomes saturated resulting in restriction of the normal circulation of air, decline in the level of oxygen and increase in the level of carbon-dioxide". The position has emerged as a result of rising water-table in respect of area growth of different categories of water-logging conditions in the Indra Gandhi National Project command Stage-I.

It is evident from Table 20 that the potentially sensitive areas when water-table lies between 1.5 to 6.0 metre below ground level is approximately 74,000 hectares in 1981 has increased to 3,12,711 hectares in 1997-98 which is approximately more than four times. The area under critical water-logging conditions having water level 1.0 to 1.5 metre which was about 22,000 hectares in 1992-93 has increased to more than 11 times (253471) in 1997-98 and where water level is less than 1.0 metre has increased from 13,750 to 18.087 hectares during 1992-93 to 1997-98. The main factors responsible are liberal use of canal water for irrigation and recharge of ground water.

Table 20

Water-logged Area (I.G.N.P)

Year	*Water Level (mbgl)* Water logged area less than 1.0m*	*and Water logged Critical Area 1.0 m of 5m*	*area (ha)** Potential sensitive 1.5m-6.0m*
1981	—	—	74,000
1991	—	—	2,02,700
1992-93	13,750	22,000	2,92,960
1993-94	9,680	17,760	1,60,760

1994-95	10,192	18,970	1,98,643
1995-96	14,750	20,600	2,07,300
1996-97	17,220	24,140	2,97,820
1997-98	18,087	25,347	3,12,711

*metre below ground level`**. Hectare

(b) Salinity of Water—The soluble salts present in the land get dissolved in excess water collected on the land. These salts are concentrated on the surface causing soil salinization. The increase in salinity affects the vegetation.

The similar problem exists at the Chambal command area in Hadaulti region. The area of Bundi, Arnetha, Kapren and Laban before canal irrigation facility was quite barren. The people used to offer milk instead of water as the water was so scare. The canal irrigation has changed the total scenario of the area which became full of food crops, sugarcane, etc. The water level has risen considerably and people used to draw water by hand from the wells. The happiness lasted for a few years and the farmers are now worried as the land has become quite useless even for the previously growing crops in the area.

The use of mechanical tools have also changed the land structure to some extent as these tools completely over turns the land and destroy the inner land structure which holds the roots of the vegetation. The traditional way of ploughing only shuffles the soil without provoking the inner layers of the land.

The use of mechanical tool, chemical fertilizer and electric power for irrigation has added to the cost of production considerably and the selling price is in the hand of middle man, and thus the farmers by and large suffer. Almost 90 percent farmers in India are having only pieces of ploughable land cannot afford these facilities as they do not get the returns. The failure of electricity and power cut again a headache. A large quantity of water is wasted by using motor pump for irrigation where water does not percolate through out the soil as it does in the traditional way of irrigation.

Mineral Resources

India is rich in mineral resources and has the potential to become an industrial power. It has large reserve of iron ore, extensive deposits of coal, sizeable quantity of mineral oil, rich deposits of bauxite and has a virtual monopoly of mica. The country is still deficient of some minerals like petroleum, tin, lead, zinc, nickel, etc. There is continuous search and exploration of mineral wealth which has yielded promising results, thus adding to the known and potential deposits of various minerals. However, the mineral wealth is not uniformly distributed. The Northern India is almost devoid of any known deposits of economics minerals. Whereas north-eastern parts possess large number of minerals like coal (three-fourth of country's total), iron ore, mica, bauxite and radioactive minerals.

The mineral wealth is an important non-renewable natural resource which forms the basis of development of the area. The unscientific and excessive exploitation may ever become a reason for disaster in the area.

Energy Resources

The economic and industrial development of a country depend upon the energy resources. The parameter of development is the quantity of energy consumption by a country, more energy consumption means more development as the energy is required for all the human activities. The energy resources should be developed and conserved in order to keep pace with the developed countries. The energy is not endlessly renewable, once it is consumed it is lost forever. The energy should be used very carefully as all the forms of energy are ultimately converted into heat energy. India has three major resources of energy viz., coal, petroleum and hydroelectricity. The other energy sources which supplement the requirement are atomic energy, bio-gas geothermal energy, natural gas, solar energy, tidal energy, wind mill. The production and distribution of important energy resources is as follows—

Coal

Coal is among the most important traditional source of energy and accounts for about 67 percent of the countries commercial requirements. Resources wise, coal occupies the pride place in the inventory of mineral resources in India. India ranks third in the world after China and USA. The major coal deposit states are Andhra Pradesh, Assam, Arunachal Pradesh, Bihar, Chhattishgarh, Gujrat, Jharkhand, Madhya Pradesh, Maharashtra, Meghalaya, Nagaland, Orissa, Rajasthan, Tamilnadu and West Bengal. The total known reserves of coal are estimated 234.11 billion tonnes.

The coal production of country was barely 32.8 million tonnes in 1950-97 which has increased upto 300.63 million tonnes in 2000-2001 and is the fifth largest coal producing country in the world. The entire production of coal is under the public sector which is organized by Coal India Limited with its seven subsidiaries.

Oil and Natural Gas

The Assam and adjoining areas were the only oil producing area till independence. It made headway only after independence, more particularly over the past tow decades. Oil is critical to India's economy, which stated with a modest level of indigenous crude production of only about 0.25 million tonnes in 1950-51 and reached to 32.428 million metric tonnes in 2000-01. The production of natural gas which was 18.3 billion cubic metres per day in 1993-94, increased to 29.48 billion cubic metre per day in 2000-01. The Government is also taking measures to stop flaring of gas resulting in increased availability of this 'Green Fuel' to power projects, industries and even to homes through pipe lines.

The petroleum industry is entirely in the public sector which is organized by "The Oil and Natural Gas Commission" with its 12 subsidiaries. The commission has recognized 26 basins having the deposit of fossil fuel. The total oil area is about 14.1 lakh square kilometers, 85 per cent lies on earth and rest 15 per cent on sea side. The estimated total reserve of oil and natural gas is approximately 620 crore tonnes.

Hydroelectricity

There are many multipurpose projects in the country which have helped in fulfilling many much desired objectives like irrigation, controlling floods, checking land sliding, solving drinking water problem, development of transportation means, etc. Above all of these, the main objective is power generation to meet the increasing demand due to increase in human activities which require ample power.

The power plays a key role in the industrial, agricultural and commercial sectors of the economy and is also the most crucial source of domestic energy supply. The power requirements of the country is met through the network of hydro-electricity, thermal and nuclear power stations. Thermal electricity is, however, the largest source of power supply. The performance of power sector has been quite encouraging. Gross power generation has gone up from about 56 billion kwhs in 1970-71 to 420.622 billion kwhs (Bu's) and recorded 6.6 percent rise in 2000-01. The largest share about 80 percent has been contributed by thermal power plants followed by hydel power 18 per cent and nuclear power 2 percent of total power generation. However, there remained power shortage. The gap between the demand and supply which was 12.6 per cent in 1980-81 came down to 6.1 percent in 1980-81, but again rose to over 13 percent in 1993-94 and there is a trend for increase in next following years. Initially, the industries were the largest power using sector and consumes about almost-half of the total power supply in the country. However, with the modernization of agriculture and urbanization, the break up of power consumption is 30—40—30 ratio for industry; Domestic Agriculture.

The hydel power which contributes about 18 percent of energy requirement of the country is produced by constructing dams on all seasons rivers and by rotating the turbines by sharp and powerful jet of water current. The advantage of hydel power over fossil fuels and nuclear power is that it does not cause pollution and mostly unending type where as the fossil fuel, and nuclear power generation cause pollution and the sources are limited which are likely to be finished. The disadvantage of hydel power generation is that it depends upon water which is mostly due to rainfall.

Nuclear Power

A large amount of energy is obtained from nuclear fuel. Tata Institute of Fundamental Research has started the 'Atomic Energy' programme. The Atomic Energy Commission was established in 1948 with sole objective to produce power and utilization of atomic energy in the field of agriculture, industry and medicine.

Conclusion

The average consumption in Rajasthan was 3 units/day/ man which has now crossed 100 units. The thermal power plants, hydel projects and nuclear power plants contribute 40.3, 39.6 and 20.1 per cent respectively. There is now much demand because of increased human activities in the fields of agriculture, industrial, commercial, etc. sectors and due to use of many power operating domestic appliances like air conditioners, refrigerator, washing machines, micro-oven, television etc.

The conventional sources like coal, petrol, natural gas are limited and cannot be used in large excess for more power generation because of environmental problem, so is the case with nuclear energy which emit radioactive rays in the atmosphere which remain for a pretty long time damaging the ecosystem of the area.

The hydel power is pollution free but requires all seasons flowing rivers and sufficient rains to keep the required water level for rotating the turbines as such dependent and not reliable.

The solar energy and wind mills may prove a better alternative as Rajasthan is receiving abundant radiant energy from the sun and eminently suitable for power generation through sun and wind. These sources seem to be quite fascinating as there is no operational cost involved. Anyhow, environmental impact must he considered.

The last but not the least choice is bio-gas plants which will not only provide a cheap source of pollution free energy by contribute to economic aspect too. The common people belonging to villages may be involved and trained for proper implementation, working and maintenance of the bio-gas plants.

Population Explosion and Urbanization

The first ever census of country was conducted in 1872 but 1881 census is a official recognized date as it was made methodically and in accordance with law. The census is now conducted after every 10 years, the last census was made in 2001, the counting period has been 9th February to 28th February 2001 and reference date is kept 1st March, 2001 at Sunrise.

In terms of the size of population, India is the second largest country in the world, next only to china. The population of India (1,027 million; 1st March, 2001) constitutes nearly 16.89 per cent of the world's total estimated population of 6163 million. India supports approximately 17% of the world's population and 20% of the cattle of the world with only 2.42 per cent of the world area (135.79 million square kilometers). The country is facing difficulty to support the huge population on so small an area with barely two percent of the total global income.

Population Size and Growth Rate

The population size and growth rate is quite unprecedented and causing anxiety which is represented as under.

(i) The population of India which was 23.8 crores in 1901 and showed a slow growth till 1921, reason being semi-balance between birth and death rate.

(ii) The period between 1921-1951 has increased constantly because of control of droughts and epidemics resulting the decrease in death rate and birth rate more or less remained the same.

(iii) There is a population explosion between 1951-1981 because of better health care, the death rate has continuously decreased and the birth rate has been stabilized.

(iv) The period between 1981-2001, the population has increased but the growth rate has declined. The people were concerned to keep small family.

Birth and Death Rates and Life Expectancy

The average birth rate in India declined from 412 per thousand during 1961-71 to 372 during 1971-81 and the death rate also showed a similar decline from 19.2 to 15.0 per thousands during the same period. The average birth rate was 31.7 against death rate of 11.0 during 1981-91 whereas in 1991-2001, the birth rate is projected at 24.8 as against the death rate of 8.9. It is expected that the stabilisation of population in India would be obtained by 2025 if the present trend continues. The life expectancy has also arisen from 37.1 (male) and 36.2 (female) in 1951 to 62.3 (male) and 65.27 (female) upto the end of 20th century.

Population Growth Rate

The decennial growth rate of population is 21.34 percent during 1991-2001 in comparison to pervious decade 1981-91 which 23.85, decrease by 2.51 percent. The census figures indicate that the average annual growth rate in population has fallen to 1.93 per cent during 1991-2001 as against 2.14 percent during 1981-91. It is estimated that even at this rate of growth, India will overtake china by 2050 to become most populous country in the world with a share of 17.2 percent. India with a population of over one billion as on May 11, 2000 has already joined the "Billionaire club" along with China, China has registered a growth of just 1% very much close to USA with 0.9% world's third most populated country against the world population growth of 14%. Kerala showed the lowest decadal population growth rate at 9.42 percent, while the Nagaland is highest rate of 64.41 per cent. Andaman and Nicobar showed a dramatic decline growth rate from 48.70 in 1991 to 26.94 percent in 2001.

Literacy

The literacy rate has shown an increase from 52.19 percent in 1991 to 65.38 percent in 2001, it was only 36.11 percent in seventies. The literate male, female ratio showed 75.85 percent (male) with 54.16 percent (female) in the country which was 46.77:24.88 in the seventies. Kerala topped the list among the states with 90.92 percent literacy rate, first in the country both in male (94.20%) and female (87.86%). Mizoram is next with a literacy rate 88.49 percent. The lowest literacy rate is Bihar with 47.53 percent preceded by Jharkhand which has literacy rate of 54.13 per cent.

Though the literacy rate has improved but the picture is quite unsatisfactory, even after 57 years of independence, the condition of literacy is so poor that out of 67 crores of voters, 48 crores are illiterate which is approximately 72 per cent of voters. Really it is a tragedy and very sorry state of affairs for a democratic and independent country like India.

Density of Population

There were 324 people per square kilometre in 2001 as against 267 in 1991, an increase of 46 persons per square kilometre during the 1st decade.

The population density of a place depends upon the factors like land structure, climate, rainfall, nature of soil besides economics, social and cultural conditions and security of life and property.

Most Populous State

The Uttar Pradesh is a most populous state with a population of 166 million, which is more than the population of most of the countries of the world. The four countries Brazil, China, Indonesia and U.S.A. have large population than Uttar Pradesh.

Urbanization Trends

Urbanization is most dynamic process, almost half of the world population is already in Urban areas. It is estimated that by the first quarter of the 21st century, majority of the world population will be in the 'Urban Settlement'. The process of Urbanization through which population settles within are as classified as Urban, has different trends in the developed and developing countries. The process of urbanization process in highly industrialized countries has already reached to high level by the middle of the 20th Century and has now stabilised. By the year 2025 almost 80 percent resident of these countries will live in cities and towns.

The trend of Urban population growth has indicated that the number of cities with population of 1 lakh and above (class 1 town) has increased from 74 in 1951 to 296 in 1961 and population showed to increase from less than 3 crores to over 6 crores during these forty years whereas the bigger cities with population of 10 lakhs and above recorded a still sharper rise and the number has increased from 12 to 23 and population from four crores to over seven crores during the period 1951-1991.

Rural Settlements

The 1981 census show that there are 5,57,137 inhabited and 48,085 uninhabited villages in India. Uttar Pradesh has the highest number of villages (1,12,566 habited and 11,680 uninhabited), Madhya Pradesh has 71,352 villages while Sikkim has only 440 villages.

Tribal Settlements

It is mostly found in the forest areas and the nearby haunts. The total tribal population of India was 67.8 million in 1991.

Population Policy

The population problem in India is a matter of grave concern and has serious implications for socio-economic progress. The present population not only hampers the economy of the country but affects the welfare of future generation.

The National Population Policy (NPP) which is announced in February 2000 with sole objective of achieving a stable population by 2045 consistent with economic growth, social development and environmental protection. National commission with Prime-minister as chairman has been set up having state chief ministers, central members. The guidelines are—

To Improve

(i) The mode of contraception,

(ii) Health care infrastructure,

(iii) Basic reproductive and child health care, and

(iv) Total Fertility Rate (TFR) to replacement level of 2.1 by 2010

Environmental Impact of Growing Population

The growing population along with urbanization process has serious environmental consequences affecting the natural resources. The huge population require more water, food and fuel on a larger scale not found in nature. The problem of urbanization is more serious as nature cannot provide resources needed to support life, neither it can disperse the waste produced by large population. Apart from this, the problem of continuous and unsystematic growth of urban population include chronic housing shortage resulting squatter settlement and slums, widespread poverty, environmental degradation and increase in delinquency and crime. The fact is that every city has two type of populations, one well housed and provided with a variety of services and amenities and the other ill-housed and are deprived of the basic facilities. Between 30 to 40 percent of urban dwellers in developing countries are poor are live in slums as shanties.

There are many slum areas in and around major cities. The slums occupy mainly municipal disposal areas and are located on steep hill sides, which are deprived of even basic amenities, housing space, potable water and means to clean their surroundings. The pity is that the all the municipal waste collected from different parts of the city is being dumped at these places resulting health problem. The authorities who are responsible to clean the surrounding of a city make these areas full of rubbish materials, thanks to a few persons who take round in early hours of morning to pick up some useful material and earn their livelihood.

There are many other environmental problems associated with growing population and urbanization. These problems includes water, air, waste and disposal of toxic and hazardous waste. Lack of sewers or other means to dispose of human excretes safely and insufficient garbage collection services which add to water pollution problem because the uncollected wastes are washed into main streams.

Air pollution is also a serious problem. There are four major sources of air pollution which are:

(i) Industries

(ii) Fuel for heating and electricity generators

(iii) Solid waste disposal

(iv) Motor vehicles

The growing population also encroach on rich agricultural land in the surrounding areas. According to FAO estimates about 1.4 billion hectares of arable land in the world has been removed from agriculture between 1980 and 2000. The forest land has also been encroached for agricultural and other activities. It is estimated that is 4-lakh hectares of forests were brought under cultivation, and another 8.56 lakh heactares were cleared for other uses like cities, roods, industries. More than 12 lakh hectares, 79 per cent deforestation is attributed to population growth.

Social and Cultural Impact

Most of the developing countries witnessed economic recessions but population growth remained high. These countries have no option but to take loan from the international monetary fund on stringent conditions resulting drastic reduction of investments in health, employment, educational and technical development of the country. These restrictions affected the environment in three ways:

(i) Declination in real income and quality of life.

(ii) Benefits from earlier social development programmes gradually disappeared

(iii) The increasing capitalization market has become the basis of social relation relegating human considerations.

There are several social repercussions of such changes in the basis and method of evaluation of social relations. The resources are developed for the benefits of the dominant people and dominant regions for instance, the aim of the Tehridam in the Himalayan region is to provide water to farmers of the plains of downhill. This dam will submerge forest and agriculture land and will disable people from their age old habitat. It has been estimated that 18.5 million persons have been displaced due to construction of large dams and only 4.6 million of them could be rehabilitated. Lack of public awareness fails to compensate the deficiency.

The development, by nature, has created a situation of 'internal colonialism' that means, resources of poor regions are drained to the developed regions without giving proportionate benefits to source regions.

There are many dimensions of human development. The basic necessities of human being are food, cloth, house, education, water, medical facilities etc. are some of the important necessity of the mankind. The satisfactory supply of natural resources play an important role in the development of human society. There will be enough discontent and anarchy within the society if the supply and demand of the resources are not proportionate, which ultimately would cause a bad effect on the environment.

The census of 2001 has indicated that there is no appreciable change in the growth rate in comparison to other countries of the world but the natural resources of the country have not increased in comparison to the population growth. The situation is quite alarming and difficult. The challenge is to be met by all sector of human society and every individual has to play an active and important role.

The natural resources like water, minerals, forests, etc. have been exploited badly in order to meet the demand of growing population. This tendency has polluted every segment of the natural resources. The urbanization process along with industrialization have produced many pollutants and solid wastes, deforestation for more land, encroachment into arable land, excessive burning of fuels for more power, are some of the reasons for environmental degradation because of growing population and urbanization. The water resources are being utilized for domestic purpose instead of irrigation. There is a great pressure for effective transportation system in the cities.

The growing population and urbanization has led to many social evils too. The employment avenues have not increased in proportion to growing population. In addition to this, labour oriented works have been greatly reduced due to mechanization of industrial activities resulting unemployment.

The Government has spent much amount in education sector and people has developed aptitude towards education. The educated unemployed young people are more frustrated, leading a secluded and anarchical life. The social evils like murder, rape, molestation, terrorism, crimes in urban areas is due to these frustrated and highly educated young people who have been trained and called as future makers of India. The defect is in the framing and implementing the education policy which is much more oriented towards the direct employment. There are thousands of qualified engineers, doctors, MBAs, professionals, etc. are jobless yet many technical colleges have been opened just to add more frustrated educated young man into the fray of existing lot.

The society is adopting single family concept instead of joint family yet there is no appreciable change in the traditional way of life because of sense of insecurity between the different section of the society. There is a competition amongst the family members, each individual member has developed a tendency to work for himself. The young people do not take care of their old parents who have sacrificed all their pleasures to make the life of their dependents on the plea that it was a duty.

The growing population and urbanization has also developed a mixed culture society. The means of transport has connected far distant places and people have easy access to any part of the country. This has changed the total concept of 'born here and die here'. The people of different parts of the country with different culture and way of life have assembled at a place where they have an opportunity to earn their livelihood. This has led to some extent as a good gesture amongst the people and developed brotherhood but ultimately resulted in rivalry. The people has lot the sense of humanity. The neighbours live like a stranger and no body is worried about other's distress. Every one of us is uncle and aunty of the rest. The young generation more or less adopted the western culture and the old generation is bound to support. The western culture is fast changing and believed in fast life, fast food, and enjoy the life for own self. The young people celebrate 'Mother's day', 'Father's day', 'Valentine day'. 'New years day' and remember these days but are unaware of their own important festivals. The new trend has begun recently the Dandiya, Garba, Bhangra Dances etc. are performed collectively on Holi and Diwali which have no relevance with the festival.

Conclusion

The growing population and urbanization have led the developmental programme. The environmental problems by the developmental programme lead to the conclusion that the development and environmental degradation are two faces of the same coin and go side by, if head wins, tail loses and vice-versa. Despite this, neither developmental activities can be ignored nor degradation of environment is allowed to continue. Thus, there is urgency to strike balance between them. The destruction of environment is due to wrong perspective and family planning and management. The people by a large thinks of 'common property resources' as of government. There is always a tendency for maximum exploitation of resources to fulfill the individual interests, assuming that the responsibility of management lies with the government.

People hardly care for environmental conservation if socio-political restrictions are not imposed. The urgency is to involve people and impart. 'Environmental education' which will help in creating environmental awareness among the people, increased efficiency and training specialists to tackle environmental problem. The environment conservation is not a single handed work, it needs equal partnership and involvement of each individual person as it cannot be solved by any government or agency without the co-operation of the masses. The steps which should be taken are—

(i) Use natural resources with care and frugally

(ii) Change the life style

(iii) To respect and honour the dedicated persons in the mission

(iv) To reward the person contributing in the conservation of environment

(v) The educate children and make them responsible

(vi) To take care of natural resource of area.

5

Sustainable Development of Water Resources

Definition of Sustainable Development

The satisfaction o human needs and aspirations, is the major objective. The essential needs of vast numbers of people in developing countries—food, clothing, shelter, jobs- are not satiated beyond basic levels and the people develop legitimate aspirations for an improved quality of life World in which poverty and inequality are endemic will always be prone to ecological and other crisis. Sustainable development requires meeting the basic needs of all and extending to all, the opportunity to satisfy their aspiration for a better life.

Living standards that go beyond the basic minimum can be sustained, if only consumption standards are conceived on a long-term basis. Yet, there is an inbuilt contradiction in the use of world's ecological means, for instance, the patterns of energy use of World's ecological means, for instance, the patterns of energy use, irrigation etc. The need identification must be socially and culturally anchored, and sustainable development requires, promotion of values that encourage consumption standards—within the bounds of the ecological possible and to which, all can reasonably aspire.

Meeting the essential needs, depend in part on achieving full growth potential, and sustaining the development which clearly requires consistence with economic growth, provided the clearly requires consistence with economic growth, provided the content of growth reflects the broad principles of sustainability and non-exploitation of weaker section of the population. High levels of productive activity should be conterminous with sustainable development.

An expansion in numbers can increase the pressure on resources and slow the rise in living standards in areas where deprivation is widespread. Though the issue is not merely one of population size but of the distribution of resources, sustainable development can only be perused if demographic developments are in harmony with the changing productive potential of the ecosystem.

A society may in many ways compromise its ability to meet the essential needs of its future generation – by over exploiting resources. The direction of technological development may solve some immediate problems but lead to even greater ones. Large sections of the population may be marginalized by ill-conceived development priorities.

Growth has not set limits in terms of population or resource was beyond which lies ecological disaster. Different limits hold for the use of energy, materials, alter and land. Many of these, will manifest themselves in the form of any sudden loss of a resources base. The accumulation of knowledge and the development of technology enhance the carrying capacity of the resource base. But, ultimate limits their area and sustainability requires that long before these are reached, equitable access to the constrained resource and re-orient technological efforts to relieve to the pressure are to be ensured.

In essence, sustainable development is a process of change in which the exploitation of resources, the direction of investments, the orientation are all in harmony and enhance both current and future potential to meet human needs and aspirations.

Weighing Costs and Benefits

Addressing environmental problems require not that discount rates be artificially lowered but rather that the value of the environment be factored into decision-making. Values that are difficult to measure are often implicit in decision-making, but the tradeoffs are not well thought through. There is a clear need to make such costs and benefits as explicit as explicit as possible so as to better inform policy makers and citizens. This does not imply that is possibly, or even desirable to put monetary to know how much environmental resources. But it is desirable to know how much development is being given up in the name of environmental protection. It is argued that too much environmental quality is now being given up. There is, however, a danger that too much income growth may be given up in the future because of failure to clarify and minimize tradeoffs and to take advantage of policies that are good for minimize tradeoffs and to take advantage of policies that are good for both economic development and the environment.

To clarify these tradeoffs at the national level, efforts are under way in a number of countries to amend the national accounts. Such exercises can be valuable for two reasons. First, they can help indicate how growth of GDP may bring with it environmental costs for today's citizens. For example, the costs of pollution to health and productivity should be taken into account in the same way that other measures of welfare need to be considered. Second, it can help give a more realistic measure of the capacity of an economy to produce. To this end, investment has to be adjusted to take account of depreciation of physical and natural capital but the accumulation of human capital and the benefits of technical change must also be taken into account to provide an overall picture of an economy's productive capacity.

A Preliminary Review of Impacts made by Large Dams-World Bank

Large dam projects are controversial. Thus proponents point to the social and economic development benefits that dams make possible, by providing electric power, irrigation for agriculture, and residential and industrial water for growing towns and cities. Critics consider that project sponsors and financiers systematically downplay the deleterious effects that dams can have on displaced people and the environment. They argue that there are usually cheaper and more benign alternatives to meet the same developmental goals.

World bank has examined the outcomes of 50 completed large dams assisted by the bank[2].It finds that the projects have a mixed record in their treatment of displaced people and in their effects on the environments, but that the policies the bank has adopted on resettlement and environmental aspects of projects have improved performance" on the ground". In most of the cases reviewed, benefits have far outweighed costs, including the costs of adequate resettlement programs, environmental safeguards, and other mitigatory measures, These results suggest that the bank should continue supporting the development of large dams provided that they strictly comply with bank guidelines and fully incorporate the lessons of experience.

Development Benefits

The 50 dams reviewed have made major contributions to economic development. They have created an installed power generation capacity of 39000 MW and they replace the equivalent of 51 million tons of fuel in electric energy production annually. They control floods and provided water for urban population and for industrial development b. they have extended irrigation for another 1.8 million hectares, substantially increasing cropping intensity and yields of major food crops.

In Pakistan, for example, the directs benefits from irrigation made possible by the Tarbela and Mangle dams are estimated at about $260 million annually. The added supplies of irrigation water have made it possible to grow the equivalent of two wheat crops a year on 400,000 hectares of previously irrigated land 400,000 of previously rain fed land. Indirect benefits are difficult to qualify. But an impact evaluation shows that farmers with irrigated land have increased their incomes and are spending them on consumer goods and on education, including for girls. The increased farm activity generates demand for associated industries such as fertilizer production and agriculture output processing.

Social and Environmental Impacts

Resettlement

Resettlement has been inadequately managed in half the projects:

Overall, the 50 dams have displaced about 830,000 people. Based on information in bank a report, the outcomes of resettlement have been satisfactory in 25 of the large dams (involving 540,000 people), unsatisfactory or unknown in 24projects, and no resettlement was required in one projects. However, mo0st projects, and no resettlement were required in one project. However, most projects predate the bank 's resettlement guidelines, and often, judgment on outcomes are largely based on the views of the implementing agency rather than on audits to establish whether displace people's income have been restored to pro-project levels, as required by today guidelines.

The resettlement results of recent projects are better than those of projects approved before the guidelines came into force: of the dams appraised since the first resettlement guidelines were issued in 1980,relativelyfew have been completed and evaluated, but it appears that the guidelines have improved performance; of the 14 completed and evaluated dam projects appraised since the guidelines were issued, resettlement has been unsatisfactory in two (Kedung Ombo in Indonesia and Kiamberer in Kenya).

Problem with resettlement and compensation of indigenous people appear to have been frequent: many dams are in remote whose people have a social and cultural identity that is district from the dominant society and makes them vulnerable to being disadvantages by development. Unfortunately, because most of the projects in this review were approved before the Bank's

Guidelines on indigenous people were issued in 1982; few of them recorded information on the condition OED impact evaluations and reports by other agencies point to this as an outstanding issue for the Bank and its borrowers.

Environment

The Bank's guidelines now provided that any project-included environmental degradation must be avoided, mitigated, or offset as part of project design and implementation. It is too appears early to judge compliance with the new standards, but it appears that many problems identified by the OED review are more prevalent in early projects than in recent ones.

The 50 dams have mixed records on the management of environmental consequences.

In area where tropical waterborne diseases are endemic, new reservoirs can add to health risks successfully at moderate cost many have mitigated losses to fisheries by creating new fisheries within the reservoirs, and few of the dam projects have enhanced areas for wildlife. Concerns about the loss of natural habits have been raised in connection with 13 of the projects, only two of the which appear to have taken adequate mitigatory measures,. In two cases (Bayano in Panama and Kariba between Zambia and Zimbabwe) major irreversible degration of a pristine nature habits has been reported. The adverse impacts on habits in the other 11 projects have in general not been large or irreversible.

Water degradation and downstream effects. Watershed degradation, loading to sedimentation of the reservoir, sometimes accompanies the building of a demand the opening up of a area to settlement and deforestation. These problems have affected the viability of only one of the dams (Kulekhani in Nepal), but in another 8 projects they are serious enough to warrant continued monitoring. Where increased water logging and salinity and other adverse effects have occurred downstream do dams, they have usually been the results of inadequate complementary investments rather than of problems in herent in the dam projects themselves.

Benefits versus Costs

The large majority of the dams received are yielding benefits that for outweigh their costs of adequate measures to mitigate their adverse impacts. Among the 50 dams built, 45 are yielding acceptable benefit/cost ratios. Adding the probable cost of measures that the projects could have taken to satisfy today's guidelines on resettlement and the environmental makes little difference to the estimates returns.

In almost all other cases, mitigation measures, including appropriate resettlement programs, could have been financed without jeopardizing the dam's economic returns. Thus by today's standards, and based on the available information, 13 of the 50 dams can be regarded as acceptable, 24 as potentially acceptable and 13, all appraised before 1985, as unacceptable.

Preliminary Lessons

- *It is never too early to consider social and environmental issues.*

The damage caused by adverse social and environmental impacts is much greater than the cost of mitigation. The potential social and environmental impacts of projects need to be considered—on the basis of detailed reliable information—starting at the planning and pre-feasibility stage.

- *If a project is economically justified, an adequate resettlement program and adequate measures to mitigate environmental impacts are likely to be readily affordable.*
- *Institutional capacity and commitment are crucial.* With enough commitment, knowledge, and resources, the adverse impacts that have occurred could have been prevented, reduced, or offset. Careful assessment of the responsible agencies capacity and commitment to manage the social and environmental aspects of a project, and adequate provisions to ensure their satisfactory performance, need to go hand in hand with concern about physical magnitude such as the area of habitat to be flooded or the number of people to be resettled.
- it may be approved for the Bank to require an *ex ante environmental and resettlement assessment for all dams that is might assist, directly or Indirectly—much as it already requires safety evaluation.* This would provide an opportunity to identify additional mitigatory measures as needed, and to require these measures to be implemented as a component of Bank support.

Emerging Problems in India

The emerging problem have been aptly described in reports of CSE

This is briefly described below:

Whatever the central Water commission (CWC) may argue, more and more experts are beginning to question the very utility of big dams and especially of the large surface irrigation schemes they offer to the country, In a study on canal irrigation and its impact on crop production and environment. Dr. Bhumbla, Former agriculture commissioner and vice-chancellor of Haryana Agricultural University, argues "from the experience of major and medium irritation works in India, it is evident that its benefits in arid areas though spectacular for the first 10-20 years, gradually get reduced and a considerable portion of the land gets deteriorated because of water logging and salinity. In the humid areas, the benefits are doughnut from the beginning and in many cases negative. The envisaged for future in humid areas, in my opinion, would not only lead to disastrous consequences in degradation of soil and environmental, but would also results in reduced agricultural production, It is time to halt the expansion of these programmes..........."

In low rainfall areas of Rajasthan and similar areas of Punjab and Haryana (300 mm to 400 mm), canal irrigation is necessary because raising crops like cotton in the kharif season and wheat in the Rabi. In semi-arid regions of Tamilnadu, Andhra Pradesh and Karnataka, where rice and sugarcane are the main irrigated crops, increases in yields have been significant.

But in all these areas water logging and soil salinisation have emerged as serious problems. As far as unlined canals and distributaries are concerned, a study by the Central Water and Power Commission in 1967 revealed that about 71 percent of the water is lost in transit from the reservoir to the field.

Loss of water from unlined seepage (percent)

Canals	15
Distributaries	7
Watercourses	22
Field Losses	27
Total Loss	71

Increasing Waterlogging

The water table in the Bhakra canal command area has been rising at the rate of about one meter Year[3]. The managing director of the Haryana states minor Irrigation and Tube Well Corporation in a press conference in late 1983-expressed serious concern over the raising groundwater table in the state. He said that 65 percent of the area in the state covered by canal commands had saline groundwater aquifers underneath and in 4 lakh hectares; the water table had entered the critical zone of up to 3 meters depth. This was creating water logging accompanied by salinisation.

The rising water table will affect the production of many crops adversely. The story of canal irrigated areas pf Pakistan where cotton has vanished from many fields is likely to be repeated, save Bhumba. The high water table, apart from affecting agriculture productivity, has many other adverse effects because of the loss of moisture storing capacity of the soil, even slight rains cause floods. The maintenance of roads and building becomes difficult and diseases increase because of water logging. In Hissar in Haryana, the load bearing strength of the soil has become less than 50m percent in 15 years.

In the sub-humid and humid areas of the country (rainfall more than 1,000 mm), Bhumbla argues that the benefits of canal irrigation are questionable of canals has resulted in reduction in many areas, introduction of canals has resulted in reduction in productivity of crops .In Bihar, Madhya Pradesh and orissa, which together have2.5 million hectares of canal irrigated area, and where rice is the main irrigated, but there has been no perceptible increase for the past 20 years[3].in Uttar pradesh, which has the maximum canal irrigated area, there is a general complaint that in the canal irrigated area, apart from pre-sowing irrigation,hardly one irrigation is possible and the wheat crop frequently suffers from moisture stress.

During the drought of 1979-1980,the farmers in the sarda sahavak command area complained there was no water in the canal but in the wet year of 1978,the canal water aggravated the flood problem created by the excessive rain, in the rice growing area, water is seldom available for raising rice nurseries before the start of the monsoon rains. Thus, in the non-rainy season, winter or summer, when irrigation could in significant increases in yield enough water is not available.

Further, in the humid areas, it becomes difficult to manage canal water during the rainy season and the problem of water logging becomes serious in a much shorter time. In fact, this may aggravate the problem of drainage and result in loss of production.

The situation is likely to be much worse as canal irrigation is introduced in high rainfall areas particularly if the soils have low permeability as has been demonstrated by the situation in Tawa and Barna command area, where yields of all crops have declined since the introduction of canals. Bhumbla therefore concludes. "The effect of canal irrigation on increasing cropping intensity is marginal". He argues that the irrigation departments do not even produce relevant data to show the cropping intensity in land irrigated by canals and tube wells. All that we know is that in 1976-77, the net irrigated area was 34.8 million hectares and the gross irrigated area was 43.1 million hectares, which gives a cropping intensity of 1.24 which is very low and a good reason for the low productivity of irrigated lands in India.

Bhumbla argues that in most canal-irrigated areas cropping intensity is less than that in tube well irrigated areas. Bhumbla argues that the government should concentrate on ground water development areas in small reservoirs instead of canal irrigation schemes.

Dams and Forest

A large dam inevitably alters the course of nature and, because of the play of complex and largely unknown forces; the ecological consequences are usually much more than were bargained for. Silent Valley has been dropped but the government has decided to go ahead with tehri, Sundar Sarovar, Vishnuprayag and many other projects. Also being proposed is the Manibhadra dam in Orissa, in one the prime forest areas remaining in the country.

The forest cover bears the burnt of dam construction in more than one way. In the Himalayan an valleys, contractors who come to clear the forest which is going to be submerged greedily cut trees even in unaffected areas. People who are being displace from Tehri town in Garhwal to make way for the dam will be rehabilitated on forest land that has been acquired and cleared near Hardwar and Rishikesh. The forest is also being cleared for storage of construction material. With the reduction in forest increases. Their need for firewood leads ton further denotation. The construction of a dam, therefore, has a multiplier effects

The 1983-84 annul report of the department of environment revels that the construction of the Idukki dam over the Periyar river in kerala has hastened the degradation of vegetation sharply reduced the forest cover. It is estimated that during the period 1951-1976, 0.49 million hectares of forest has been due to major river valley projects. This is roughly 10 percent of the area that came under canal irrigation –5.5 million hectares.

Despite the increased awareness about the need to protect forest cover, little attention is paid to this factor when a site is selected for a dam, basically, because all forest s are state property and no has to be compensated for them. Even in cost-benefit calculations, forest loss is grossly undervalued and the recurring loss in terms of timber and firewood yield per year and social costs of degradation of environment are never taken into account. Under valuation of standing forest helps in boosting the cost-benefit ratio for obtaining Planning commission approval and finance form international agencies like the World Bank. Moreover, the contract for clearing the forest is also undervalued, thus leaving a bigger margin to be shared between the contractors and the forest department.

Because of public protest some provision is now made for reforestation or compensatory afforestation.

Alternative to Big Dams

Storage of water by building large dams is regarded by irrigation engineers as a crucial component of India's water management system. The Central Water Commission argues that benefits like hydroelectricity, irrigation, flood control, industrial and municipal water supply are not possible "unless the water is stored in reservoir created by dams". Water storage is necessary because rainfall is very unevenly distributed, varying form 10,000mm in Cherapunji to about 100mm in Western parts of Rajasthan. There are also considerable seasonal variations. Over 75 percent of the rainfall is received during the monsoon period of June to October and even during this period there are many erratic spells of heavy rain and dry weather. On one hand, as many as 99 districts are classified as draught-prone; 85 percent to 90 percent of the monsoon water flows waste to the sea.

Since independence, about 700 storage dams have been constructed. The total storage capacity created so far, including those of small tanks is assessed to be about 16 million hectare meter. Out of a total of 178-mham surface water available in the country, only 27 mham are now bemg used and the utilizable potential is about 67 mham. About 90 percent of water being used is for irrigation alone.

By the year 2000, the Government hopes to provide irrigation to 113 million hectares, the ultimate irrigation potential out of a gross cropped area of 200million hectares. Major and medium irrigation projects would irrigation project 54.6 million hectares. Between 1980 and 2000, some Rs.60000 crore (at 1980 prices) will be required for the development of this irrigation potential. At the beginning of the sixth plan a total potential 0f 56.51 million hectares had been created of which 26.61 million hectares was through minor irrigation. By June, 1984, about 65.5 million hectares of irrigatin potential had been created.

Potential Capacity

As even by the year 2000 nearly 40 percent of cropped are will be unirrigation, the government is preparing a national perspective plan for water resources development, which will allow for large scale inter-basin resource development, which will allow for large scale inter-basin transfer of water from water surplus river basins to water scarce river basins. This will mean that an additional 22 mham can be utilized, but this inter-basin transfer of water will again depend primarily on the creation of storage reservoirs: the ultimate storage capacity in the case has been assessed at 37.5 mham.

The irrigation potential will thus increases from 113 million hectares to148 million hectares coming under surface schemes and about 10 million hectares benefiting from increased use of groundwater. This ambitious plan will require an investment of about RS.50000 crore. The investigation and planning work of the development of the perspective plan will cost Rs. 107 crore spread over seven to 10 years.

The commission argues that if water resources have to be harnessed by building storage reservoirs then either development areas with a large population, agriculture areas, of forest areas with a large population, agriculture areas, of forest areas with a tridal population have to be submerged "If none of these are to be affected we may have to stop all further progress in water resources development".

Thus, if government programmes go head as scheduled, there will be hardly any free flowing rives left in the country,. Already the cauvery is fully exploited. The Krishna and Godavari rivers, with large dams like "Tungabhadra, Srisailam, Nagarjunasagar, Mula, Jayakwadi completed or near completion and several new rivers in the offing like Ichampalli and Polavaram should be fully exploited soon with the award of the Narmada Tribunal, the Narmada Valley Development Programme has also been launched and by the early part of the next century, the Narmade will bre a fully controlled river. The Tapti with Ukain and upperTapti dams will soon become a fully used river. Mahi with Bajasagar and Kadana dams faces the same prospect, and so does the Betwa with Paricha, Dhukwan, Orchha, Matatila and Rajghwat dams.

Lessons of Indian Experiences and Sustainable Water Resources Development

A study was carried out by CWC and details of the quality of life of the Indian people. Since the Improvement of the quality of life of the Indian people since the country's independence in 1947. Water resources projects have been major contributors towards economic growth in India. However, there has been some apprehension that benefits from these projects may not be sustained over along period if environment considerations are ignored. The development and management of water resources is handicapped by the lack of appropriate guidelines and an attempt is herby made to provide them.

The past four decades have been a period of unprecedented water resources development in many developed and developing countries. Most of the large dams (more than 15 m in height) were constructed during this period. Water resources projects of various sizes were built to provide water and power needed for development and economic growth. Now, many environment al lessons can be learnt from the operational experience from different parts of the world. Some of the lessons are:

- In the assessment of environmental impacts, attention has mainly been given to the negative impacts; the positive impacts should also be looked into the maximized;
- It has seldom been verified whether the predicated environmental impacts have come true; even if predictions were not made in old projects such verification or evaluation is essential to make reliable prediction in future and to suggest remedial measure for past omissions;
- Disease have spread after completion of large water resources projects primarily because of lack of awareness and infrastructure to prevent and combat the diseases, proper epidemiological investigations and quantitative data on incidence of water related disease should be done and
- Overall estimates are often based on guess and rough estimates; they need to be replaced by factual data and computations.

Adam moderates floods (advantage) but reduces river flushing and flood lain nutrients (disadvantages!). A water resources projects enhances availability of water (advantage) but may substantially increase the risk of transmission of water- borne diseases (disadvantage). Thus, water resources projects, like all other type of major development projects, contribute to many desirable and undesirable environmental and social effects. These projects were often planned and designed in the past without explicitly taking into account the complex inter-relationships that exits between people, water and other related natural resources, biota, environment in general and various development processes.

A wide variety of subjects are of significance in major water resources projects—physical science such as hydrology, water management, water management, land use and agricultural development; biological science such as forest, wildlife and fisheries; social science such as rehabilitation, human health and general poverty allviation .All these issue have a bearing on the overall environmental quality both directly and indirectly.

In recent years much public attention has been focused on the dependence of development activities on the careful planning and management of natural rescues for indicate that it is necessary to examine a number of problem areas in order to ensure that environmental concerns can be effectively integrated in the both directly and indirectly.

Often, the basic environmental information for the projects area is not available. There must be a good database, detailed guidelines manuals, trained manpower and good mechanism for monitoring the environmental effects.

Water Resources Development and Environmental Effects

The development of water resource requires planning, designs, construction, operation and management of facilities to control and utilize water efficiently, while these aspects have been traditionality in the domain of civil engineers, the services of service of specialist from other disciplines are indispensable.

Water resources development requires constructions of structure which can control water flow effectively into structure is often a dam which divides the environmental into upstream side comprising the catchments, reservoir and the dam the downstream side comprising the command area and water distribution system. Other common structure required for the effective control of water are following (Linsely and Franzini, 1979):

(*a*) Storage reservoirs to retain excess water from periods of. High flows for use during the period of low flows. By moderating the floods peaks, flood damage downstream of the reservoir can also be reduced

(b) Water delivery systems to transfer water from reservoirs to fields

(c) Diversion structure (pipes, flow dividers and other engineering facilities) to ensure effective operation of the systems;

(d) Intake structure and distribution systems to meet municipal and industrial water demands;

(e) Collection and treatment of sewage and industrial and agricultural effluents, and their environmentally safe disposal and

(f) River engineering works to stabilize river reaches including estuaries.

Broadly, four types of environmental effects of water development may be recognized:

(i) ecological aspects;

(ii) environmental pollution aspects;

(iii) change in physical and chemical parameters, and

(iv) impacts on living beings.

It should be noted that the environmental effects of water resources development are complex and interrelated, but they are very real. Indeed, as water development is intensified, almost new hydrological conditions and a anew kind of environment emerge. Some of the environmental impacts and relationship among water, land and people are illustrated. These can, however, be effectively planned and managed through a close integration of natural applied and social science, which could eventually to equitable sharing of benefits and sustainable development.

Environmental Impacts Assessment

In the past, problems created by water resources projects have drawn the attention of planners and the general public to the environmental implication of such projects. As early as 1950, the issues related to health, fisheries and settlements were identified. In the last sixties recognition of the full network of ecological impacts were stressed within the context of river basin planning. The Environmental Impact Assessment (EIA) techniques were introduced in the 1970s. Our knowledge base and understanding of environmental impacts have increased steadily during the past two decades Consequently, environmental assessment procedures and technique have become progressively more rigorous over the recent years.

The United States of America (USA) enacted the National Environmental Policy Act (NEPA) in 1969, thus became the first country in the world to adopt legislations making environmental impacts assessments mandatory for major development projects. Since the introduction of EIA in 1969, mo of countries have already enacted in the process of enacting, EIA mandatory. Such legislations should be compatible with the legal, economic, social and technological framework as well as appropriate to the expertise available in such individual country.

At present, there are many variations in the definition of Environmental Impact Assessment (EIA) concept is still evolving, and is likely to evolve further with time. Normally EIA. Is considered to include

- An assessment of the environment effect of a development activity;
- a prediction of he changes in environment quality which could result as direct and indirect consequence of that development activity;
- an attempt to consolidate the environment effect to a common basis, with economic costs and benefits, inter comparison purpose;

- Comparison of various alternatives by which desired objectives can be realized and identification of the alternative option which could optimize economic and environment benefits as compared to the costs, and
- An implement able plan for management and monitoring of environmental quality during and following the construction of the project.

To take care of the above mentioned aspects, it is necessary to identify the elevate parameters, collect and process required data, interpret the result of the analyze with insight and sensitivity, and present the conclusion and recommendations in an easily understandable, comprehensive and recommendations in an easily understandable, comprehensive and standardized format .ELA is essentially a decision – making tools. It provided information on relevant manner. The process is future-oriented and thus attempts to predict the environmental consequences of the proposal development alteration (UNEP, 1988). When properly carried out. ELA provides a comprehensive evaluation perspective for making rational decisions.

Sustainable Water Resources Development

Environmental sustainable water development and management of water implies the following considerations

(a) development is managed in such a way as to ensure that resources are conserved and /or restored, and that beneficial environmental effects are maximized while the adverse effects are ameliorated to the extent possible.

(b) efficiency in the use of water and capital is a key criterion in the selection of strategy, and

(c) option for future development are not foreclosed.

Technical improvements are increasingly directed towards, for the same level of technology, sustainable may have different connotations. Alert ion is mainly to be given to achieve sustainability commensurate with the general development is shown

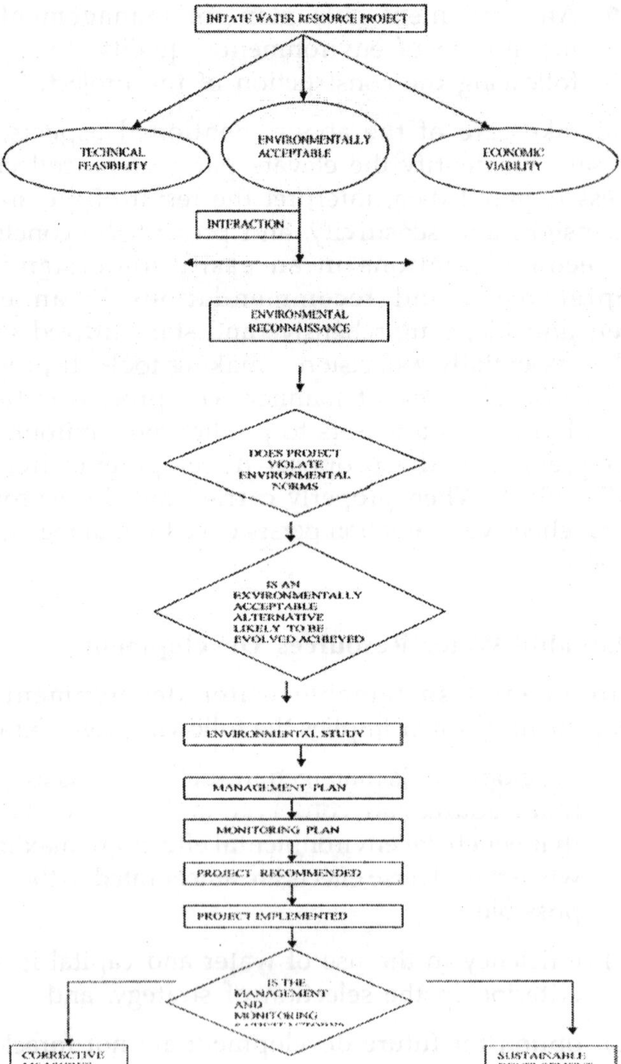

As indicated in the figure, three studies have to be carried out for a new water resources projects, namely, technical feasibility, environmental acceptability and economic viability. There should be close interaction amongst these studies; the environmental acceptability for sustainable development is taken up to ensure that the project impacts are within the supportive and assimilative capacities of environment. For this purpose, an environmental reconnaissance is carried out. If environment reconnaissance shows that violation of environmentally acceptable alternate is to be abandoned. In case such norms are not violated or an alternate is found feasible projects –feasibility and environmental studies are taken up which, inter-allia, include environmental management and monitoring programmes. These activities have to be received, checked and corrected for achieving sustainable development. Unfortunately for many of the projects currently under operation, such detailed approach was not followed.

The past as mentioned in earlier chapters, not only in India but also in all other developing countries, ex-post monitoring and evaluation of water projects have received virtually no attention .For sustainable water resources development, this situation has to be remedied on an urgent basis.

Preparation of monitoring and environmental plans some basis requirements. These are the following:

(i) Timeliness;

(ii) Cost-effectiveness;

(iii) Maximum coverage

(iv) Absences of bias, and

(v) Identification of users of information.

Following variables that need to be monitored are listed as per the guidelines prepared by CWC.

(a) Water Resources, including Quality: Monitoring measures are required for the following:

- Change in the quality of surface and groundwater;
- Sediment depositing rates and patterns;
- Change in ground water levels;
- Water loses from reservoirs and canals due to seepage leakages and other reason;
- Reuse of waste water;
- Efficient use of water in various sectors for better water conservation, and
- Status of eutrophication of the reservoir and the river.

The water quality of surface and groundwater should be monitored once in a month for the certain. The Ground Water levels should be monitored in the wells of the command area.

The data collected by Central Ground Water Board can also be utilized. The Project Authorities on the Basis of these data can prepare ground water table contours and specify the area under the risk of water logging.

In addition to above quality of waste discharged into surface water should be monitored at all points. The Minimum number of points recommended is:

(i) Upstream site where water is clean;

(ii) Stream just below source of pollution or dilution;

(iii) The location where stream is at worst condition due to a specific source, i.e. bottom of oxygen sag curve; and

(iv) Stream at a appoint midway between bottom of oxygen sag curve and recovery of oxygen level.

From time to time the measurement for seepage and

evaporation must be done as per IS: 8414 and 6939 respectively.

(a) Water Supply and Sanitation

- Quality of available drinking water, and reliability of the supply at appropriate locations during each season;
- Quality and extent of waste water treatment and its disposal, and
- Percentage of population having sanitary facilities, and their potential impacts on ground water quality.

(b) Water Logging and Drainage

- Water table fluctuations in command area;
- Areas under the risk of water logging
- Status of implementation of drainage system as planned

Effectiveness of drainage system installed;

- Salinity of drainage water;

Other water quality aspects of drainage water and

- Rational reuse of drainage water.

All these should be carried our for each check. The drained water should be analyzed for SAR, EC, Residual Sodium Carbonate, Nitrogen, Phosphorus and Pesticides.

(c) Soil and Appraisal of Soil Salinity

The nutrient content of soils namely Nitrogen (N), Phosphorus (P_2O_5) and Potassium (K_2O)as well as micronutrients namely Zinc (Zn), Copper (Cu), Iron (Fe), Manganese (Mn) should be monitored at the beginning of each cropping season and the general does of application of fertilizers; both chemical as well as organic shall be calculated depending on the nutritional status of the sol and the type of crop grown. This will facilitate to:

- Maintenance and/or enhancement of soil fertility in the project area;
- Efficiency of structural and agronomic measures taken for soil conservation and erosion control, and
- Monitoring of PH, ESP,EC of soil before and after the cropping seas change soil before and after the cropping season

(d) Land Use

- Change in land use from one category to another should be monitored once in five years through satellite imageries;
- Impacts on soil and water due to change in land use practices, and
- Change in land–holding patterns by usual observations followed if necessary, by perusal of records.

6

Statistical Evidence of Environmental Perception

Statement of the Problem

Not only that the slums create pollution through their unorganized and unsystematic waste and sewage disposal congested and unsystematic as well as through unethical socio-cultural habits and values, but in a fact these slums are created only on already polluted places due to their convenience in occupying unauthorized land. The slums are generally created on the side of sewage drains, garbage disposal places and on unused waste land at the public and community places. Hence the slums are doubly polluted which resulted their life into miserable unhygienic and unethical. This not only has adverse effect on the present day working people, but also destroys the life positions of the youngsters and children, the future working population. Not only that the work efficiency and physical health is affected but also that it imbalances the mental and psychological equilibrium of the people in these communities which in turn damage the socio–cultural as well as physical environment of other city dwellers.

Increasing pollution due to slums and in slums have been the major concern of to days government for any urban development planning. Programmes, plans and strategies are being developed to remove these slums by shifting them to other safe and better planned places whereever it is possible. Simultaneously it is also essential to make the present slums tolerably livable by providing essential services and educating them for following environmental ethics.

In order to develop a realistic plan for managing the polluted slums. It is essential not only to provide essential services and educational opportunities but also to know the present status of pollution more especially in respect of the perception of dwellers. The environment cannot be pollution free unless the dwelling community perceives the need for it. It is in the respect this study was postulated to find out the perceptions of both males and females. About the different kinds of pollution in their area and the extent of need to improve up on.

Objectives

The present study was conducted in one of the slum area of Delhi to find out the perceptions of the dwellers in respect of different types of environmental pollution and their consequences on various aspects of their life.

- To study the socio-personal characteristics of the respondents from slum area.
- To study the environmental perception of slum dwellers with respect to air pollution water pollution housing environment pollution personal hygiene pollution , noise pollution, light pollution and socio-cultural pollution.
- To study the perceived consequences of various kinds of pollution on the life of the dwellers such as on physical health mental health, occupational

efficiency, income social relationship, habits and social values and personality development.

Limitations of the Study

Being a student's research it had the limitation of the money and other resources. The study was made and the data were collected only by a single researcher which made the area limited. In view of this the finding cannot be generalized for all the slum areas. Further the reliability of the data as in other social science studies depended on the validity and reliability of the responses provided by the respondents.

Population Distribution Over Native Place

People from different states have migrated and settled in this slum community to earn a living. Some of the people came to Delhi as visitors and later decided to stay here. These people visit their native place regularly. About 32% of the population has come to the community from Uttar Pradesh, 26% are from Bihar, 28% from west Bengal, 6% form Bangladesh and Haryana and 2% from Maharashtra.

Housing

There are three type of jhuggis in the community. Some are kuccha some pucca and some semi pucca.

About 62% of the Jhuggis are of semi-pucca type. About 32% are pucca and less number of Jhuggis i.e. about 6% of the Jhuggis is kuccha.

Drainage and Sanitation

About 66% of the drains in the slums community locality are open and 34% are closed. Sanitation in most of the jhuggis is either average or poor. People are least concerned about the sanitary conditioned prevailing in the community.

Occupation

About 42% of the people gainfully employed comprise of junk dealers, 18% are employed in private service, 14% are shop owners only 5% are government employees and 14% work as labourers.

Common Place of Gathering

There are various places in this slum community where people gather for group talk or discussion. These places are the deepalaya school, youth club, Pradhan's site, tea stall and at somebody's house.

Educational Status

The educational status of the people is not good. About 38% of the populations are illiterate. About 40% of the population have studied till primary, 10% of the population have studied till middle school, 9% till high school and the rest 3% are intermediate and graduates.

Educational Distribution Over Sexes

The rate of illiteracy is high among females as compared to male. About 12% of the males are illiterate. 53% of the males have studied till primary school, 16% have studied till middle school 15% till high school, 3% have studied till intermediate and 1% is graduates.

About 79% of the females are illiterate. 20% of the females have studied till primary school and 1% has studied till middle school.

Health Services

The various health services that are used by the people are through private clinics in Srinivasapuri, Lajpat Nagar, Kalkaji and East of Kailash; Safdarjung hospital, AIIMS, MCD Dispensary in srinivaspuri and Kalkaji; and through doctors who visits the community for health check ups.

Immunization Status

Most of the children in this slum community are partially immunized. Only 7% of the children are fully immunized. 53% of the children are partially immunized and about 40% of the children are not immunized.

Among male children 12% are fully immunized where as not even a single female child is fully immunized 36% of female are partially immunized.

Selection of the Respondents

One hundred fifty respondents were decided to be selected from the TRN J.J. Camp community by simple random sampling technique.

There are approximately 800 households in the TRN J.J. Camp community. Every fifth house hold was selected with random start to reach 150. Only one member of the family and that also a person above the age of 18 years was interviewed.

Variables

Variables included in the study were selected on the basis of extensive review of literature and discussion with and guidance by advisor.

The independent variables which were included in the study were:

Age

Sex

Religion

Caste

Educational status of respondent

Family income

Family size

Main occupation of family

Family education status

Family type

Duration of stay in the locality

Original place of residence

Type of house

Number of rooms in the house

Mass media exposure

The dependent variables which were required to be included in the study to meet the objective were:

Environmental perception

Air

Water

Housing environment

Personal hygiene related items

Noise

Light

Socio-cultural pollution

2. Perception of consequences of environmental pollution

Definition and Measurement of Variables

Proper conceptualization and operationalization of variables are indispensable ingredients of scientific research because they enable researchers to measure them (Kerlinger 1973).

Definitions of the variables of the present study and the procedure followed for their measurement are as under.

Independent Variables

Age

Age of respondent was operationlized as the calendar years of the life completed on the date of interview/

Bhagat (1983) defines age as the number of full years completed at the time of data collection. Respondent above the age of 18 years were selected for the study.

Sex

This variable was dichotomized into male and female. Male and female respondents were given the following numeral code:

Sex	*Numerical code*
Male	1
Female	2

Religion

Chamber's English–Hindi dictionary has defined religion as particular system of faith in worship of a supreme being or God/Gods.

The respondents belonged to Hindu, Muslim, Sikh and Christian religions.

Religion	*Numerical code*
Hindu	1
Muslim	2
Sikh	3
Christian	4

Caste

Caste is an endogamous and hereditary subdivision of an ethnic unit occupying a position of superior or inferior rank or social esteem in comparison with other such subdivision (Kroever, 1930)

Caste is related to the status of an individual in the society by birth. The respondents were categorized into four caste groups;

Caste groups	*code*
General (like Brahmin, Thakur etc)	1
OBC (Like Jaat, Kohli etc)	2
SC (Like Balmikijan etc)	3
ST	4

Educational Status of Respondents

It refers to the formal education received by the respondents in the school and colleges. Education helps an individual to acquire knowledge and skill and it gives shape and direction to the thinking process.

Jhamatani (1986) defines educational level as the type of school where maximum years were spent the level up to that the individual had studied.

Rao (1988) defines education as the respondents educational qualification acquired through formal schooling.

In the present research education has been operationalized as the number of years of formal schooling successfully completed by a respondent.

Category	*code*
Illiterate	0
Just literate	1

Primary	2
Middle	3
Up to matric standard	4
Above matric	5

Family Income

Family income includes the total monthly income of the respondents and family members from all the sources.

The respondents were asked to the state their monthly income through all sources.

The responses of the respondents were categorized as follows

	Category	*code*
1.	Below 500	1
2.	500-1000	2
3.	1000-1500	3
4.	1500-2000	4
5.	2000-4000	5
6.	2500-3000	6
7.	3000-3500	7
8.	3500-4000	8
9.	Above 4000	9

Family Size

The size of family was operationalized as the number of members (children/parents) depending upon the head of family. It refers to the number of family members living under one household.

Main Occupation of the Family

Normally occupation refers to some physical or mental activities which are relatively permanent, performed by an individual to earn a livelihood (Tirupataiah, 1989)

In the present study occupation has been conceived in terms of the head of the family.

The occupations were categorized as follows:

Category	*Code*
1. Rickshaw / Auto- Rickshaw / Taxi Driver	1
2. Footpath shop / seller	2
3. Government service	3
4. Service in company	4
5. Service to private persons	5
6. Artisans/ Manufacturer/ Processor	6
7. Junk Dealer	7

Family Education Status

It was realized that educational status of family members plays an important role in determining the way one gathers information about environment pollution.

Family education status has been operationlized as the level of literacy of family members. This was calculated as the average of the educational status score of all the members of the family.

Family Type

This variable refers to the type of family viz. joint and nuclear. The joint family constituted of spouse, their children, parents, siblings and other relatives staying together. The nuclear family comprises of the spouse and their children only.

Type	*Code*
Nuclear	1
Joint	2

Duration of Stay in the Locality

This refers to the time period for which the respondent and their family members have been residing in the locality. The period of stay was recorded in years.

Original Place of Residence

This refers to the place where the respondent and their family originally belong to i.e. the place of birth of the respondent or his parents. The data were categorized state wise.

Type of House

Type of house has been categorized in to three types. On the basis of its construction style. They are kuccha pucca and semi pucca. A kuccha house is made up of mud and clay with straw. The roof of the house is made up of bamboos. A pucca house has a wall, floor and ceiling which is made of cement and is concrete.

A semi pucca type of housing lies between kuccha and pucca type where some portion are concrete while others are not.

Type of house	*code*
Kuccha	1
Semi pucca	2
Pucca	3

Number of Rooms in the House

It refers to the number of rooms present in the respondent's house excluding kitchen, bathroom and toilet.

Mass Media Exposure

This refers to the extent to which an individual respondent is exposed to different mass media of communication such as radio television newspaper films etc.

According to Hwash (1973) the exposure to mass media refers to the degree of which a farmer makes use of mass media such as radio television newspapers magazine etc. to acquire information.

For this study the mass media exposure was considered as the score on frequency of using mass media like newspaper radio and television. The scores were given on the frequency for each media separately.

Dependent Variables

Environmental Perception

Environmental perception has been defined as the process of taking cognizance of a sensible or a quasi-sensible object, or the process of becoming aware of something. Thus environmental perception is the process of taking cognizance of the environment.

Individual and groups of people relate to environment through their perception. Their decisions and actions are influenced by perception of internal link within a problem rather on tradition customs myths awareness and stage of socio-cultural development.

Environmental perception is based on custom culture faith objectives and experience and difference from person to person. Environmental perception plays a most significant role in the management of environment. Perception constitutes a value system that constraints planning and purification. Thus the solution to environmental problems must be based on a clear perception of them.

There are different forms of environmental pollution:

Air-Related Environmental Pollution

Air pollution is one of the commonest forms of environmental deterioration in the cities of both the developed and the developing countries. Air pollution refers to those conditions in which the general atmosphere contain substance in concentrations which are harmful to man or his environment (Gilpin, 1976) or which interference directly or indirectly with mans comfort safety or health.

Various sources through which air environment is being polluted are category into:

Category	*scoring*
Fuel based items	
Industry based items	
Community based items/slum housing	
Disposal of waste related items	
Lavatories and toilets	

Water related environmental pollution

Water pollution to the deterioration in chemical, physical and biological properties of water brought about mainly by human activities.

Water pollution is the alteration in physical chemical and biological characteristic of water, which may cause harmful effects on human and aquatic life. Water pollution in most of the rivers, lakes and reservoirs of the country has increased and their water is not considered safe for human consumption without proper treatment.

The various water polluting sources are categorized into

Category *scoring*

Water drainage

Drinking water.

Use of chemicals (industry based)

Lavatories and toilets

Disposal of waste

Housing environment

Housing environment

Housing in modern concept includes not only the physical structure but also the immediate surroundings. The WHO prefers to use the term residential environment which is defined as the physical structures that man uses and the environs of that man uses and the environs of that structures including all necessary services, Facilities equipment and devices needed or desired for the physical and mental health and the social well being of the family and the individual.

To put it briefly a healthful residential environment is one in which the family can develop and flourish physically mentally and socially.

The various sources through which housing environment is polluted are'

Category *scoring*

Space in house/number of rooms

Type of house (kuccha, pucca, mixed)

Dampness in house

Nearness to sewage/stored water

Light

Slum lanes

Cots and clothes in the house

Personal Hygiene Related Items

Personal hygiene may be defined as that branch of hygiene which concern itself with the adjustment which the individual must make to preserve and improve the health of his body and mind. Thus it deals with matters which are personal responsibility of every person.

The various sources that effects the personal hygiene of person are

Category	*score*
Bathing and cleaning	
Clothes	
Drinking of safe water	
Eating of clean and fresh food	
Cleaning of teeth, mouth hair etc	
Mixing with unsafe people	
Stay in dirty environment	

Noise Pollution

Noise pollution is an added dimension of environmental pollution. The main sources of noise pollution are automobiles and loudspeakers.

The acoustic division of national physical laboratory, New Delhi has found the average noise levels of cities to be quite high.

The various sources that produce noise pollution are

Category	*scoring*
Noise of industry	
City noise	
Noise of social function	

Noise by slum dwellers

Light Pollution

One environmental aspect of transportation facilities largely ignored is that of light pollution. In many areas light pollution has become an important aspect of both planning and design.

It has been estimated by researchers that by to 50% of all light pollution may be the result or roadway lighting.

The various sources that produce light pollution are categorized as

Category	*scoring*
Natural light during daytime	
Electricity light during night	
Lantern/candle light	

Socio-Cultural Pollution

Socio pollution refers to these aspects of urban problems such as problems of residence including housing congesting on the one hand and on other hand are the problems of population such as child labour beggars exploitation and corruption family disturbance social exploitation and maladjustment .

The various sources that contribute to socio cultural pollution are

Category	*scoring*
1. Family relation disturbance	
2. Caste struggle/class struggle	
3. Political function	
4. Social evils in society	

Like drinking gambling, prostitutes, drug addiction etc.

The respondents were asked to rank the seven pollution according to their perception. Subsequently they were asked to rank the various pollutants under each type of pollution separately. The ranks were scored and the mean score for each type of pollution and for each pollutant were calculated.

Consequences of Environment Pollution

Prevention of disease and preservation of health depends to a large extent upon the environment in which people live.

Air pollution is one of the commonest forms of environmental deterioration. As a result of increased industrialization the percentage of carbon monoxide and sulphur dioxide is increasing in the atmosphere. The abated use of insecticides and pesticides and the industrial and nuclear fallouts fly ash and particulate are increasing pollution in alarming rates in the atmosphere.

Apart form creating problems of poor visibility, dust pollution causes respiratory disease. Other disease includes pneumonomiosis, silicosis and asbestosis which are caused by inhalation of dust. Eye ailments include cataract conjunctives, corneal ulcers, and squint trachomia.

Water pollutions the most important cause of public health problem both in urban and rural areas. Water borne disease such as cholera typhoid diarrhoea dysentery malaria and intestinal worms claim a hear by too of light.

Noises of modern society have an adverse impact of human health and physical system. The efficiency of a person is reduced and damaged affecting your sense organs and the nervous system. Noise can be damaging to human ear. Many emotional a behavioural problems occur apart from rise in blood pressure, mental abnormalities in foetus, headaches etc.

The perceived consequences of environmental pollution

were studied in respect of the physical health, mental health, occupational efficiency, income, social relationship, habits and social value and personality development of the slum dwellers. The consequence of each type of pollution were asked to be placed on 5 point scale, viz. does not affect, affects to a little extent, affects some extent, affects to great and completely damage; having scores 0, 1, 2, 3 and 4 respectively.

Method of Data Collection and Construction of Research Instrument

The data were collected from 150 respondents with the help of an interview schedule, specially constructed for the purpose of this study, keeping in view the objectives and variables of the study.

An interview schedule was prepared by reviewing literature and guidance by the advisor. Necessary precautions were taken to ensure that the questions in the schedule were unambiguous, clear, complete and comprehensive. The prepared interview schedule was pre tested on 10 respondents and necessary amendments and modifications were incorporated. The modified schedule was then used for data collection.

The interview schedule was designed in two parts, part-A and part-B. Part-A of the schedule include questions for gathering information on personal profile such as age, education, occupation, family income, etc. and consisted of questions to measure the extent of mass media exposure of respondents.

The second part i.e. part-B included questions to measure environmental perception of the respondents and perception of consequences of environmental pollution.

The data were collected by the researcher on the schedule through personal interview. The researcher visited the slum community and contacted the respondents. Each interview took 40 to 50 minute's time. The respondents generally provided free and frank response on almost all questions except on a few where little more probe was made and rapport was established.

Analysis of Data

The data gathered through personal interview schedule were coded, transferred on the data sheet and tabulated in respect of frequencies. The data were analysed with the help of statistical tools such as frequency distribution, percentage, mean, chi-square(x2) and zero-order correlation (?)

Formula / Mathematical equations used for statistical analysis are as follows:

Frequency

The number of observations falling within a particular class range or category is called its frequency.

Percentage

Percentage = Class frequency/total frequencyx100

Mean (average)

Mean (X) =

Xi/N

Where

ΣXi – sum of all observed values'

N – number of 12

Chi-square(x^2)

Chi square value for i X j table:

$X^2B=B\ \Sigma(Oij-Eij)/Eij$

Where i=represent row number j=represents column number

Oij – observed frequency ith row and jth column

Eij =expected frequency in ith row and jth column

Environmental Pollution

Dixon (1972) defined pollution as all those activities conscious or unconscious of human beings which detract in any way, directly or indirectly, from the enjoyment of environment and the ability to drive full benefit, there from.

Gilpin (1976) considers 'pollution' as a direct alternation of physical, thermal, biological or radio-active properties of any part of the environment by discharging, emitting or disposing wastes or substance so as to affect its beneficial use and to animals, birds, wildlife, fish or other aquatic life or to the plants.

According to a report of national academy of sciences (1980) a substances is called a pollutant if it adversely alters the environment by changing the growth rate of species, interferes with the health, comfort, amenities or property values of the people.

Sharma (1981) points out that the main causes of environmental pollution are the rapid industrialization and urbanization, use of fossil fuels, the construction of barrages and dams, the indiscriminate use of fertilizers and pesticides, and finally increasing population, all have led to depletion of forest, over congestion and waste accumulation, in totality, leading to drastic pollution of environment.

Sathyanasaijan (1985) investigated the pollutants input, rates of their distribution, pathways, accumulation sites, their enrichment, the suspended loads and sediments in the drinking water has been found to be loaded to different degree of heavy metals like cadmium, copper, iron, manganese, lead, nickel and zinc. The investigation indicated that there is a potential threat from heavy metals in the suspended load.

According to Khoshoo (1986) along with urban industrial and other development in India, the development of pollution unfortunately could not be controlled because of the insensitivity of the administrative set up which did not allow the development of a culture of pollution control.

U.N. Environment programme report (1987) reported that by the year 2000, if the present trend continue, one third of the world's productive land will be driven to extinction, and the world's climate will change, with enormous, but incalculable consequences.

Manohar Rao (1988) did a study on slum clearance and environmental improvement in Andhra Pradesh. In the study, a few major problems such as housing, food, health, employment, recreational, religious, educational and other concerned with the day to day family life of the slum dwellers are investigated here in the present study. Apart from this, the public policy on environmental improvement has been studied from its historical perspective and an attempt has been made to evaluate various programmes initiated for slum clearance and environmental improvement. Further an attempt is also made to examine the structural and functional aspects of different agencies responsible for slum clearance and environmental improvement. Finally, an evaluation is made to examine the gap between the promise and performance of the government and various government agencies concern in the matter relating to slums and environmental improvement.

Environmental Awareness and Perception

According to Lowenthal ((1967) without some understanding of the bases of perception and behaviour, environmental planning becomes a mere academic exercise doomed to failure, because they are unrelated to the terms in which people think and the goals they select.

Stone (1975) put forth this suggestion in "Should Trees have standing" that everything in the natural world has an inherent value. A common notion in eastern societies is that anything that exists has inherent value because it is the manifestation of god.

According to Karan (1977), public perception of environmental pollution of industrial areas in west Bengal among different culture brings out the importance of perception surveys in cognition of problems and approaches to their solution.

Whyte (1977) said that individuals and groups of people relate to environment through their perception. Their decisions and actions are influenced by perception of internal link within a problem rather than extremely defined objects.

Vijayaraghavan (1979) reported that the age of the participants and non-participants of IDADP had negative and significant association with awareness, while education, occupation, social participation, farming experience, farm size, economic status and overall modernity maintained a positive and significant association with awareness of IDADP among participants and non participants.

Balu (1980) found that age, education, occupation, social participation, farm size, farming experience and economic status other than cropping intensity, risk orientation and overall modernity were positively and significantly associated with the awareness of participants and non participants of the dry land agricultural development programme.

Kayastha and Yadav (1980) found that perception has important bearing on the development of flood plains dwellers of lower Ghagra Plains.

Narayan (1981) observes that the knowledge of how to protect an improve the environment through suitable environmental educational programme, is vital to the infusing of environmental education programme.

World commission on Environment and development (1987) reported that little could be achieved regarding sustainable development without reorientation of attitudes and emphasis.

Upadhyay, Chitrangad (1991) did a critical study into the possibility of implementation of environmental education as an effective remedial measure for the problem of pollution with special reference to Madhya Pradesh. The study is an endeavour to explore the possibilities inherent in the process of education which can mitigate the menace of pollution and can suggest remedial measures. The researcher feels that the process of education at various levels, formal, informal and non formal can help in the abatement of pollution and thereby in the protection of the environment.

Feijoo and Mmo (1991) studied the grasping ability of common people irrespective of instructions imparted to them. The study revealed that environmental perception correlates positively with socio-economic level of surveyed people as regardless the level of instructions (which has been included as a variable in SEI calculation). It can be concluded that the higher the level of education the greater will be the ability to perceive negative environmental factors.

Air Pollution

Dole and Hill (1950) in their study carried out in a British hospital identified patients with cancer of the lung, stomach and large bowl stated that firstly, general atmospheric pollution from the exhaust runs of the cars, from the surface dust of tarred roads and coal fires. Secondly, the smoking of tobacco is the two main causes for the above stated diseases.

U.S. National air pollution control administration (1969) examined and reported general studies in USA and Japan concluded that an abrupt rise in the concentration of smoke and sulphur dioxide in the ambient air is positively associated with excess of mortality the magnitude of which is related to the level and duration of the rise in concentration of these pollutants. The individuals most severely affected are the aged and patient with chronic bronchial pulmonary diseases and or heart diseases.

According to Gilpin (1976), Air pollution refers to those conditions in which the general atmosphere contain substances in concentrations which are harmful to man or his smoke in children in less developed countries in a cross sectional and longitudinal study conducted in New Guinea and found no consistent relationship between exposure and respiratory abnormalities.

Florey et al., (1979) are of the opinion that several researches have been conducted in recent years about the gas effect on health. In some of the students they found remarkable effect of gas on respiratory symptoms while others had no such indication. The indoor fuel produces carbon monoxide, which leads to an increase in carbon haemoglobin. The carbon monoxide and methaglobin both are detrimental to health.

Heller et al., (1979) determined the incidence of respiratory illness in households in a Midwest upper middle class community. The sample included forty-four families divided into two groups; those utilizing electricity in cooking and those using gas. Family health and demographic data were obtained from the participants. Reports of the acute respiratory illness were obtained. Ambient air was analysed indoor and outdoor in a sample of the house holds and pulmonary functions were conducted on a sub-sample of participants representing both type of house holds. The study revealed no evidence to suggest that cooking with gas is associated with an increase in respiratory disease or a decrease in pulmonary functions.

Morchandreas et al., (1981) administered their experiments on the families using wood fuel. They found that the indoor environment of such families contained more Benzo(a) Pyrine in comparison to the outdoor environment. So the researchers have come to the conclusion that the wood fuel smoke is the chief source of pollution of the indoor environment.

Spengler et al., (1983) concluded in their studies with the observation that the burning of cooking fuel produces gases such as nitrogen dioxide, carbon monoxide and carbon dioxide affecting harmfully the health of individual.

Aggarwal and Narain (1985) in their book entitled 'A Second Citizen's report' have pointed out that atmospheric pollution has for been regarded as probably the least important of all the environmental problems, connected mainly with the major cities and industrial towns. But latest evidence shows that air pollution within homes is an acute problem, an underlying cause of millions of deaths every year. The burning of cooking fuel envelops the indoor environment with heavy smoke and women who have to do all the cooking are daily exposed to more pollutants than industrial workers in extremely polluted environment. Thus, reducing indoor air pollution in poor homes is a most urgent environmental task today.

Hronec (1988) has reported about the relationship between atmospheric pollution and crop damage. Levels of dust and SO_2 concentration affect the crop.

Dave (1990) pointed out that air pollution in the capital has increased by 75% over the last decade. Particularly vulnerable are children in school buses who are caught in clouds of automobile emissions. Doctors believe that the soaring incidence of Asthma in the capital is mainly due to the increasing air pollution. Children are the most affected. Asthma can be crippling disease and deaths due to asthma are not common.

Kandapal and Maheshwari (1991) reported that biomass

fuel during its combustion produces a number of components, which are released in the environment. Carbon monoxide, carbon dioxide, nitrogen dioxide and particulate are the main pollutants of biomass combustion.

Gajendragad (1993) reported that, if at the present levels of carbon dioxide let off into the atmosphere, the Earth's temperature would rise by as high as 3 deg C by the year 2030 far in excess over the noticed during the last 1000 years.

Smith et al., (1993) selected for their study such families which used wood and gas as cooking fuel and for room heating purposes. They found that the kitchen smoke is the greatest source of indoor pollution. They also found notable difference in the nitrogen dioxide produced out of wood fuel and LPG. As a result they noted fast breathing as the main effect of indoor air pollution.

Water Pollution

Arora (1969) carried out a study to find out knowledge, habits and needs of people in relation to water. The locale of the study was a village in Delhi. She concluded that the people do not possess complete knowledge about the concept of safe water. Fifty percent population has responded positively about the relationship between water and health problems. A high percentage i.e. seventy five percent of the literate said that the characteristics of suspended matter in water cause more health problems. The population showed a satisfactory but incomplete knowledge about the types of water carrying different diseases like Cholera, typhoid dysentery and diarrhoea. Illiteracy seems to be the main reason for the lack of knowledge about the water borne diseases. The respondents have a better knowledge about the curative measures. A high percentage (forty-seven percent) of the population had no knowledge about the proper storage of water.

Tewari (1975) revealed that public hand pumps where

there was choking of sewer line, were the main sources of contamination and infection.

According to Southwick (1976) water pollution refers to the deterioration in chemical, physical and biological properties of water brought about mainly by human activities; an aquatic contamination of many living organisms or even exclusion of any form of live.

According to Deodhar and Nath (1981), water borne infections and diseases of alimentary tract constitute 60-80 percent of all illnesses in India.

Kayastha (1987) in his report on "Environment pollution in Varanasi: A study of perceptions, problems and management" stated that it is not only the successive accumulation of pollution over the years that is responsible for the pollution of river Ganga at Varanasi. It is also due to the pollution of river Ganga by the people of upstream settlements. The vast amounts of industrial urban affluent and sewage of Kanpur, reduce the Ganga water to a high state of pollution.

Agarwal (1990) measured the degradation of water soil and a few aquatic animals due to DDT residues. The study involved periodic monitoring of DDT concentration in water bottom. Total DDT concentration in water ranged from 0.062 ppb to 0.963 ppb. The total residues in the sediments samples ranged from 0.007 ppm to 0.62 ppm. The extent of DDT pollution is more at Wazirabad down stream after the Najafgarh drain has joined the river.

Arora (1990) discovered that regarding the concept of safe and unsafe water, homemakers gave the responses based on visual perception only. For safewater, forty eight percent of the respondents considered water mud as the safe water. For unsafe water fifty two percent considered water to be unsafe water.

Dakshini (1990) has clearly shown that both Yamuna and Hindon rivers are flowing above the prescribed minimal level of pollutants which is affecting the aquatic habitats of the rivers. The two rivers differ in their physio-chemical characteristics. Yamuna could be characterized by higher value of temperature, conductivity, ammonia literate, phosphates, sulphates, BOD, Copper, zinc, and nickel and the Hindon by PH, COD, DO and dissolved oxygen percentage saturation. A total of ninety two taxes were recorded dominated by cyclotellasp. Total salinity of both the rivers is similar and three times higher than the world average. Yamuna down stream of Wazirabad up to ITO tries to self purify through activities of microbes but due to continuous input of pollutants river does not show any improvement and indeed the water quality deteriorates.

Prakasan (1990) in his study on ecological, biological and pollution aspects of the Sasthamocotta Lake (Kerela) revealed that one of the main factors contributing to pollution of the lake was faecal contamination. The other pollutants, which poured into the lake, included:

- Fertilizers that flowed into the lake during monsoon;
- The loose mud that found its way into the water;
- Soaps and detergents mix used by professional washermen; and
- Waste from the filter house of the Kerela water authority.

Mishra (1991) in his study on the impact of industrial pollution form a cement factory on water quality revealed that cement dust when comes in contact with quality revealed that cement dust hewn comes in contact with water forms hydroxide which impaired natural water alkalinity. The additions of salts of Ca, Na, K and Al as hydroxides, sulphates and silicates formed varied hardness of water. All these are responsible for the respiratory and gastrointestinal diseases of the area around the cement factory.

Prasad et al., (1991) studied the pollution potentialities and physio-chemical analysis of potable water in the Bichari industrial complex is discharging in open and which migrate down and cause large scale pollution of ground water. During recent months, the quality of potable water has acquired serious dimensions and is threatening health, longevity and livelihood of the villagers.

Patel (1992) in his study, has found that the ground water quality was unsuitable for the irrigation purpose because of high concentration of chlorides and sulphates.

Remteke and Bhatacharjee (1992) studied the bacterial pollution of drinking water sources in north Tripura district. Seventy- one drinking water sources were tested for presence of bacterial pollution, whereas ring wells and dug wells are polluted. Wide spread bacterial pollution was observed in surface water sources. The significance of bacterial pollution of sources and prevalence of antibiotic resistance among coliform is discussed in the light of public health problem.

Housing Environment

Brittan et al., (1941) presented papers based on data collected by U.S. National Health Survey on the relationship between housing and morbidity variables. Frequency of illness disabling for a week or a longer was associated with degree of crowding (persons per room); rates of digestive diseases were higher for persons with no private inside flush toilet than for those having such facilities. Firstly of home incidents decreased with rising rents; incidents of common degree of crowding increased; secondly attack rates of Tuberculosis were over two hundred percent higher for persons on relief living in crowd circumstances, than for all economic status groups living in less crowded quarters (one person per room)

According to WHO (1962), in sanitary congested housing and slums could impair health in many ways and cause a number of persons of diseases.

Gadgil (1965) considers a room over crowded when the number of persons in a room exceeds three.

According Hunter (1968), the slum environment is a menace to health, safety morality and welfare of the residents there.

Dube (1973) has analysed the urban land use pattern of Agra. He has estimated that about 20 percent of the developed land in Agra is put to different types of misuse of land in the heart of the city and also in the fringe sector with a view to create a healthy and balanced urban life. However, the study ignores the fact that the market interference through which the urban trade interests is manifested usually.

According to Ramprasad (1976), solid waste may be defined as unwanted or discarded materials in solid form resulting from normal practices of the communities and it includes rubbish, street sweepings, ashes and industrial wastes.

Mohsin (1979) has provided a sociological account of the mental and physical growth of slum children of Patna. It is observed that they suffer from nutritional anaemia and calorie protein malnutrition. The correlation of insanitation and inferior growth of the child psyche has been well explained. The studies on master plan for Patna (1962) provides a comprehensive analysis of the stagnant old slums in the heart of the city and development of other slums in isolated patches in different sections where the city has showed a progressive geographical expansion.

D'Souza (1981) examines the relationship between the blighted areas and the unplanned and haphazard growth of metropolitan cities in India. He finds that one-fifth of the urban population reside in slums. 45 percent people of Ahmedabad live in slums, perhaps the highest in any city of the world.

Misra and Prasad (1990) stated that ten percent of urban solid waste is buried in sanitary landfills, the rest is allowed to spread along the roads in barren lands, in ditches and even in rivers and oceans. Today the waste has become a public nuisance because it does not and on being air pollution. It was also stated that insanitation and disease are the two main outcomes of solid waste. But more offensive are the wastes that are hazardous especially the radioactive wastes.

Noise Pollution

Vermon and Warner (1932) have found that the more task involves mental activity the greater it is disturbed by noise. They also reported the tendency as a part of work as to adopt the distracting effects of noise if continuously exposed.

Smith (1951) in his study "Intermittent loud noise and mental performance" has found that the effects upon short term mental performance of bursts of intense noise is to increase the quantity and decrease the quality of response, but the effects are of such a low magnitude that they are practically negligible.

Broadbent (1957) in his review of the knowledge relating to the effects of noise on performance has stated that the effect of high intensity, meaningless and continuous noise may appear on working efficiency in laboratory tasks, which are long and require continuous attention. The effect of noise is to increase the frequency of monetary lapses in efficiency rather than to produce decline in the rate of work, gross failures of coordination, or similar inefficiency.

Kumar and Mathur (1969) conducted a study to the see the relationship of sex with noise susceptibility. Two high sounding electric bells having the sound level of 80 db were used to produce noise in the laboratory. The two groups performed on a mechanical and a mental task requiring simple arithmetical calculation under normal and noise conditions. The females are reported to perform significantly better on the mechanical tended to deteriorate their performance under noise condition both on the mechanical and the metal basis. In the case of mental task the females did not show change in their performance under noise conditions.

Barbara (19731) notes that deafness has topped pneumonia and other diseases in the list of occupational hazards.

Vladimir et al., (1977) analyzed hearing changes after audiometric and clinical otohinolarynagological examination of a group of fifty ix, ten year old children residing near a power plant burning local coal of high arsenic content. They compared the results of both audiometric and clinical examination with those of a control group numbering fifty one children of same age living outside the polluted area. In the study it was found that in case of air conduction, important hearing losses were found at frequencies of one hundred twenty five, two hundred fifty and eight thousand Hz. Especially at the lower frequency range. While an assumed influence of the anemestic presence of middle ear inflammation is fully documented in the control group. The high statistical significance of the hearing impairments bound to points to a very low probability of their being only an accidental finding.

Cohen et al., (1980) demonstrated that with the length of residence in noisy conditions, the correlation between noise and auditory discrimination increased.

According to Kayastha (1988), Noise pollution is an added dimension of environmental pollution. The present civilization is a 'noisy civilization'.

Kak (1990) studied the effects of noise pollution on the human beings and reported that noise pollution leads to various kinds of disturbances and described them as under:

It affects hearing abilities. It has been observed that beyond 85-90 db noise affects hearing power if one is exposed to this intensity for 7-8 hours a day.

Noise pollution affects heart functioning if it is highly unpleasant and if one is exposed constantly say 7-8 hours a day to this kind of intensity.

Unpleasant sounds lead to very strange sensations as very peculiar experiences of bussing. The human ear is effected and totality of the affect spreads to the other parts of the body.

Sudden and very unpleasant noise lead to cardiac troubles—may be heart failures.

Constant exposure to noise pollution, which exists rather permanently at bus stands, industrial complexes, railway stations etc. lead to serve disturbances in auditory functioning. These can lead to impairing memory power.

Irritating constant noise pollution causes dreadful uneasiness reflected in physical and mental exhaustion sometimes intervened by or proceeded or followed by nauseating sensation.

Noise pollution, when the sound are highly unpleasant and uncomfortable lead to quicker heartbeats and thus if continuing hour lead to serious repercussions as mental tension and unpleasantness followed by withdrawal symptoms.

Noises of the extent of 90 db and more than 90 db have detrimental affects on emotional behaviours, which may be marked by aggressiveness, indifference and tensions.

Noises can impair functioning of various organs and systems of the body. It may lead to sudden changes in equilibrium of the body, physical and mental.

Very high and unpleasant noises hamper thinking powers, cause interference with cell metabolism and imbalances in the body functioning

Under the duress of constant, high and disturbing noises, respiratory disorders can be the result. Those having certain problems already are easily prone to serious disorders.

Power of retention, understanding and expression are seriously interfered, with sounds, which are of unpleasant intensity.

Disturbingly high intensity sounds affect the circulatory system in form of constrictions in blood vessels, thus affecting supply of oxygen and removal of wastages as CO_2 etc. from various parts of the body.

Socio-Cultural Pollution

Tanuja (1973) while analyzing the morphology of residential areas in Indian cities has discussed the nature and characteristic of slums. Citing the examples of kanpur and Delhi, she claims that slum development in India explained that it is the result of overcoming of overcrowding and haphazard growth of the cities. Immigrants lured by job opportunities in industrial units also take up other occupations, such as petty shopkeepers, domestic servants, milkmen, rickshaw and cart pullers and even beggars.

Vijayaraghavn (1979) in his study revealed that education, occupation, social participation, family experience, farm size, economic status, and overall modernity of the respondents have a significant and positive correlation with the awareness level. On the other side the age found to be negatively associated with the awareness regarding the IOAP programme among the participant and non-participants of the projects.

Kumar (1980) while analyzing the functionaries of Drought prone area programme found that educational status, occupational status, social participation, economic status, mass-media exposure, risk orientation, level of aspiration and economic motivation showed positive and significant relationship with awareness amongst the participants of the programme. Mass media exposure.

Varalakshmi (1985) in her study reported that T.V. is able to communicate farm and other development information to only a limited communication received from

TV to many non-viewer villagers. This enlarges the span of TV communication to a very great extent. Viewers gather different types of information through TV as agricultural practices, animal husbandry, health related programme and non conventional energy programme.

Broker (1987) showed that women acknowledged that they had learnt home management, general health, social issues etc. and this exposure raised in them, some expectancy form women's right, raise voice, against atrocities on exploitation women's right, raise voice, against atrocities on exploitation of women strength and capabilities of women as expressed by some and so called great women etc.

Hwash et al., (1987) revealed that study in a resettlement colony in Delhi and focus was on viewership and extent about the health and family welfare telespots. It was revealed that serials are the most popular programme and obtain viewership of hundred per cent. Though women do not see all the serials they watch regularly those based on religion like Ramayan, Mahabharata etc. After serials chitrahaar had viewership of ninety six per cent of the sample. Movies came third on the popularity scale having a viewership of eighty six percent in the sample. For health programmes viewership is more among illiterate (38%) than among literate (23%). Both type of programmes were watched more by older women than younger ones. Maximum viewership was for immunization spots (66%) while minimum for sanitation spots(50%). Extent of re call of selected telespots more than half of the content of telespots was recalled by the viewers showing the effectiveness of Television as the medium of education. Extent of recall was highest in family planning spots(57%) and the lowest in sanitation spots (32%). The different between the extent of recall and the variables age and education were not found to be statistically significant. The names of the disease where pronounced in English were not recalled.

Nsiah Gyabaah (1990) reported about the environmental degradation as a result on human influences on the landscape, pockets of degraded land are confined to areas of intense human activity such as farmland and overgrazed areas.

Earth is the only planet, so far known, to have an environment required to sustain life. Without environment, there is no life. Further, the quality of life depends on the quality and conditions of environment. The environmental conditions are the creations mostly by the human beings, which distracts in any way, directly or indirectly, from the enjoyment of the environment and the ability to derive full benefit there from. Pollution occurs when an unwanted and harmful substance is generated in the environment as a result of human activities.

The general environmental pollution in an urban ecosystem can be i) air pollution, ii) Water pollution, iii) Solid waste pollution, iv) noise pollution v) Social pollution. In addition to these light pollution, poverty an dunker employment pollution are some other pollution exist here and there. After having gone too far in polluting environment, man has come to realize, though very recently, that there is a need to take remedial measures.

Environmental awareness, perception and education play a significant role in the management of environment for reducing pollution. To the extent to which the citizens understand and appreciate the value of environment for aesthetic, health and happiness, they will be responsive and cooperative in safeguarding the environment from pollutants.

Not only that the slums create pollution but , in fact these slums are developed only on already polluted places. The slums are created generally on the side sewage drains, garbage disposal places and on the unused waste lands. Hence, the slums are doubly polluted.

Increasing pollution due to slums and also in slum and

also in slum areas have been the major concern of today's government of planning the urban development programmes. It is in this respect essential services on one hand and by education the slum dwellers on the other hand for following environmental ethics. The environment cannot be pollution free unless the dwelling community perceive the need for it. Unless they are aware and conscious of the consequences of environmental pollution. It is in this connection, this study was proposed to know the present perceptions of slum dwellers about the environmental pollution.

Objectives

To study the socio-personal characteristics of the slum dweller respondents.

To study the environmental perception of slum dwellers with respect to air pollution, water pollution, housing environment pollution, personal hygiene pollution, noise pollution, light pollution, and

To study the perceived consequences of various kinds of pollution on the life of the slum dwellers, such as physical health, mental health, occupational efficiency, income, social relationship, habits and social values and personality development.

The study was conducted on the slum dwellers of Thakur Rabindranathji Camp area of Srinivasapuri in Delhi Metropolitan city. About 86% of these slum dwellers have come from UP, Bihar and West Bengal. One hundred and fifty respondents (75 males and 75 females) were selected by random selection method. Only one member from the selected family having more than 18 years of age was selected.

The environmental perception was studied by asking the respondents to rank the seven major pollutants and their sources. The seven major pollutants included in the study were: air pollution, water pollution, housing environment pollution, personal and socio-cultural pollution.

Perceived consequences of these pollution were studied on physical health, mental health, occupational efficiency , income, social relationship, habits and social values and personality development of slum dwellers. The perceived affect, affects to a little extent, affects to some extent, affects to a great extent and completely damage.

Findings

1. Majority of the respondents belong to the age group of 18 to 30 years, while only one third were above 30 years. Only 5% were above 40 years.
2. Majority of the respondents were general caste Hindus. About equal number of respondents were Muslims and also Christians respectively.
3. Half of the respondents (males 35% and females 65%) were illiterates. Only 4% respondents (only males) were above High school.
4. About two third of the male respondents were married while among females more than 90% were married.
5. The respondents had various occupations. One fourth were junk dealers. About 35% had service as their occupation. Other occupation holders were: artisans -16%, footpath sellers-14% and rickshaw pullers-7%.
6. Most of the respondents were semiskilled daily wage or temporary employed having an income between Rs.1000 to rs.3000 per month.
7. Majority of the respondents have been staying for more than 10 years.

8. Most of the respondents have come to stay from Uttar Pradesh, Bihar and west Bengal in search of job.

9. Majority of the respondent's families had 4 to 6 members in their families while another 40% had only up to three members. Most of the families were nuclear families.

10. Most of the respondents had semi-pucca or pucca house, but did not have ration card.

11. About two-third had their own house while others had rented house. Most of the houses were single room house and that too with out bed or with only one bed.

12. Most of the respondents used to listen ratio and watch TV but did not read newspaper.

13. The respondents are aware and conscious of the harmful effect of pollution on physical health, except in case of light pollution. The highest perception score was found in respect of pollution of housing environment. Further, females were more conscious than males in this respect.

14. The slum dwellers were aware of harmful effect of noise and socio-cultural pollution on mental health. They do not perceive much effect of other pollution on mental health.

15. The respondents did not perceive much effect of pollution on their occupational efficiency

16. Effect of pollution on income of the slum dwellers was not perceived by the respondents

17. Slum dwellers felt that except the socio-cultural pollution, no other kind of pollution has any effect on their social relationship

18. The pollution related to personal hygiene and socio-cultural aspects was perceived to effect the habits

and social values of the slum dwellers.

19. The respondents did not perceive much effect of pollution on their personality development except in case of aspects related to personal hygiene.

20. There was not much difference between the perception of males and females on the consequence of pollution.

21. The respondents ranked fuel based items as I most for air pollution followed by waste disposal, lavatories/toilets, community based items and industry based items. Females respondents gave more weightage to waste disposal items to which they ranked I.

22. Poor drainage was ranked as I for water pollution followed by toilets/lavatories, waste disposal, stagnant water, drinking water and industry based pollutants.

23. Nearness to sewage was the first most cause for housing environment pollution followed by dampness, slum lanes, type of house, clothes and lack of space in house.

24. Bathing and cleaning was considered as most important for personal hygiene followed by cleaning of teeth, mouth and hair, stay in clean place, keeping away from unsafe people, drinking safe water and taking clean food.

25. City noise was ranked as I, followed by noise of slum dwellers, noise of social functions and industrial noise for noise pollution.

26. Dim light, i.e. candle or lantern light was considered harmful as compared to electricity light and natural light. The respondents were not aware and conscious of light pollution.

27. Social evils were ranked I, to create socio-cultural

pollution followed by caste/class struggle, family relations and political rivalries. Female gave more importance to family relations than caste/class struggle.

28. Income, size of family, literacy level and frequency of reading of newspaper and TV watching had positive effect on perception of pollution indicating that the respondents with higher income, large families, more literates in their families and reading the newspapers more were more conscious about the effect of pollution.

29. Period of stay had negative relationship with the perceived consequence indicating that more the stay lesser the respondents were conscious of pollution. They become used to the conditions.

Conclusion

The slum dwellers were quite aware and conscious of the harmful effect of environmental pollution on their physical health. Light pollution was, however, not considered as much harmful for them. They were aware of the effect of socio-cultural pollution on their mental health and habits and social values. Noise was perceived to effect only the mental health of the dwellers. Staying in unhygienic conditions, the slum dwellers do feel that the water stagnation, sewage, open toilets and lavatories, waste disposals and fuel based items contribute most to air and water pollution.

The respondents did not perceive much harmful effect of pollution on their occupational efficiency, income and personality development. Further, it was also found that more the people stay in slums, less they become conscious of pollution.

Implications

Developments of any kind for a community is not the sole responsibility of the Government. It is the equal and rather more responsibility of the people who live in that community. Unless, the slum dwellers are aware of and conscious of the harmful effects of environmental pollution, nothing much can be done to improve the conditions of the slums. It is in this connection essential to make the slum dwellers aware and conscious of the harmful consequences of pollution. For them, earning the livelihood is the primary need and unless they feel that their income and occupational efficiency are also badly affected by polluted environment, they will not show much interest in improving he conditions of slum areas. Hence, and educational programme is required to be launched in the slums for making them aware and conscious of consequences of environmental pollution.

Bibliography

Books and Articles

Acreman, M.C. 1996. "Environmental effects of hydro-electric power generation in Africa and the potential for artificial floods ". J. CIWEM.

Agarwal, M, C., Agarwal, R.P. 1978. Some constraints for efficient irrigation water utilization in canal command area financing agriculture.

Agarwal, V. 1978. Utilisation of irrigation potential. Economic crises.

Anthony Bottrall, 1981. Comparative study of the management and organization of irrigation projects, World Bank, 1981, p. 10.

Benerjee, M.K., 1981. A System theoretic appreciation of the command area development programme. *Decision.*

Bhatnagar, O.P., 1978. Management of Agricultural extension under T&v system in India-An overview. *Journal of Rural Development.*

Bhawan, B.D., 1984. Differential income impact of public canal irrigation in Maharashtra. In, N. Pant (Ed). *Productivity and Equality in Irrigation System,* New Delhi.

Bilgrani, K.S and J.S. Dattamunshi 1985. Ecology of river (patina-farrakha)

Bilwas, A.K. 1997. Water resources: Environmental planning, Management and development.

Bottrall, A.1978. Technology and management in Irrigated Agriculture. ODI review.

Bottrall, A. Action Research Towards Improved Water Distribution. Oversea Development Institution Network Paper 81/2.

Bottrall, A. 1981. Comparative study of the management and organization of Irrigation Projects. World Bank staff working paper No: 458,Washington, World Bank, May.

Bottrall, A.1983. An Approach to evaluating the organization and management of large Irrigation schemes. In K.K. Singh (Ed.). *Utilization of Canal Waters: A Multi-disciplinary Perspective on Irrigation*. New Delhi, Central Board of Irrigation and Power, Publication

Bottrall, A.1983. Comments on management structures for Irrigation. London; overseas development institute, ODI Irrigation management network paper

Bottrall, A.1984. Managing Large Irrigation schemes: A Problem of political economy. London, Agricultural Administration Unit, overseas Development institute, Occasional Paper 6,1985.

Bottrall, A.F.1981. Comparative study of the management and organization of Irrigation projects, World Bank Staff Working Paper.

Central Pollution Control Board 1987-90. Ganga Basin Report.

Central Pollution Control Board. 1989-90. Basin –sub basin Inventory Water – The Krishna Basin pollution.

Central Water Commission. 1968. Water resources of India, New Delhi.

Central Water Commission. 1992. Guidelines for sustainable Water Resources Development and Management.

Central Water Commission, 1997. The Kosi River: Its Morphology and Mechanics in Retrospect and Prospect. Vol. 1.

Central for Science and Environment: (1984) State of India's Environment Second Citizen Report, New Delhi.

Center for Science and Environment, 1997. The Challenge of the balance –The environmental economic in India, New Delhi

Cornea, M M. 1997."Hydropower Dams and social Impacts. A Sociological Perspective," World Bank Environment Departments Social Assessment Series

Chambers, R 1977. Men and Water: The organization and Operation of Irrigation, In B.H. Farmer (ED). *Green Revolution? Technology and Change in Rice–growing Areas of Tamilnadu and SriLanka.* London, Macmillan and Basing Stoke.

Chamber, R.B. 1984. Irrigation Management: Ends, Means and Opportunities. In N. Pant (Ed.). *Productivity and Equity in Irrigation Systems.* New Delhi, Ashish Publishing House.

Chamber, Robert, 1988, *Management Canal Irrigation,* New Delhi, Oxford & IBH Publishing Co. 1988,

Chambers, R. In search of a Water Revolution: Questions for Canal Irrigation Management in the 1980s. Water Supply and Management.

Corey, G. L. 1986. Improving Irrigation Management: Institutional and Organization Issues. In Coward E.Walter JR. (Ed.). *Irrigation and Agricultural Development in Asia: Perspectives From the Social Sciences,* Ithaca and London, Cornell University Press, 1980.

Dalua, A.K. 1993. Environmental Impact of large reservoir projects on human Settlement.

Dhruva Narayana, V. V. and Ramababu. Estimation of Soil Erosion in India, *Journal of Irrigation and Drainage Engineering*.

Edward Ries. 1974. *The Ganga, A Personal Encounter.*

Fearnsidde, P. Hydroelectric dams in the Brazilan Amazon as sources of green house gases, *Enviromental Conservation* (1995).

G., Sastry and V.V. Dhruva Narayana. Watershed Responses to Conservation Measures Journal of irrigation and drainage, *Engineer.*

Goldsmith, E, and N. Hildyard. The social and Environmental effects of large dams. Three volumes (Wadebridge, U.K,: Ecological Center, 1984-91).

Govardhan, Veelapatti, 1983. *Environmental Impacts Assessment of Tehri Dam.*

Goodland Robert. 1994. "Ethical Priorities in environmentally Sustainable Energy Systems: The Case of Tropical Hydropower". In W.R. Sheaed., *Energy Needs in the Year 2000: Ethical and Environmental Perspectives* (Canton Mass: Watson Publishing International.

Gunnar Hagman E.T. The Swedish Red Cross Stockholm & Geneva. May 84, "Prevention Better Than Cure: Report on Human and environmental Disasters in the Third World.

Halsinkum J George. Columbia University Seminar Series.

Hashmin Ali, Practical Experiences of Irrigation Reform, Andhra Pradesh In: LAN Caruthers (Ed.) *Social and Economic Perspective on Irrigation Management.*

Hashim Ali, S. 1984, One season of Integrated Water Management in Andhra Pradesh, London, Overseas

Development Institute,

Hashim Ali, S., 1986, Planning And Implementation OF Measure to Ensure Productivity and Equality in irrigation System. In, N. Pant (ED.). *Productivity and Equality in Irrigation Systems*. New Delhi, Ashish Publishing House.

Hunter, J.M., L.Rey, K.Y. Chu, E.O. Adekolu-John and K.E. Mott. 1993. Parastic Diseases in Water Resources Development: The need for Inter sectoral Negotiation (Geneva World Health Organization).

IUCN- The World Conservation Union & the World Bank, 1997 Large Dams, Learning from the Past looking at the need future.

The Indian journal of Public Administration vol XXXXIX, no. 3 July–Sep. '93- Ashish Kolhari, Is sustainable development desirable and possible.

Jayaraman, T.K., 1979. Strategies for Water Management in Command Area Development Policy and Administrative.

Jayaraman, T.K. 1981. Impact Study of an Experimental Rotational Water Distribution Scheme at the farm Level in the Mahi – Kadana Irrigation Project, Gujarat state India, Agricultural administration.

Jayaraman, T.K. 1981. Water use efficiency and rotational water supply at the farm level: certain results from an experimental pilot project in Gujarat State, India. *Water Supply and Management*.

Jayaraman, T.K. 1980. Implementation of warabandi or rotational water supply. *Management in Government*.

Jayaraman, T.K.1979. Statagies for water management in command areas. *Development Policies and Administrative Review*.

Jayaraman, T.K.1977. The citizen and water management: A case study of command areas. *Admistrative Change.*

K.S. Valdiya, Accelerated erection and landslide-prone zones in central Himalayan Region.

Lenton, R. 1980. Field experimentation and generalization in irrigation development and Management. London, overseas development institute, AAU irrigation Management Network paper.

Lenton, R. 1984. A note on monitory productivity and equality in irrigative system. In N. pant (ed). *Productivity and Equality and Irrigative System.* New Delhi, Ashish Publishing House.

Narayana, G., 1986. Farmers involvement and irrigation development: A study of warabhandi system in a villages settings in Siva Mohan, M.V.K., (ed).

P.C. Mishra and R.K. Trivedi, 1993. *Ecology and Pollution of Indian Lakes and Reservoir.*

Palanichami, K. 1984. *Irrigation Water Management- The Determinants of Ccanal Water Distribution in India: A Microanalysis.* New Delhi: Agriculture Publishing Academy.

Pant, N. 1984. *Productivity and Equality in Irrigative Systems.* New Delhi, Ashish Publishing House, 1984.

Patnaik, N. and. S.S. Virdhi, 1962. Field infiltration studies on Doon valley, *Irrigation and Power.*

Pritam singh, A.S. Ramanthan and V.G. Ganekar, proceeding of a international association of hydroecological sciences. *Flash floods in India.*

Sirkande, K. 1974. *Agricultural administrative in Andhra Pradesh,* Bombay Popular Prakashan.

Sharma, V.K. 1985. *Water Resources Planning and Management.*

Singh, K.K. Organisonal requirement for command area development in Siva Mohan.

Singh, K.K. 1989. Irrigation management by formers: the Indian experience's, SCI Journal management.

Sitapati, P. 1989 *Concept of Command Area Development in India,* Water and Land Management Training Institute, Hyd.

Stiff. (1980). *River Population Control.*

Siva Mohan, M.V.K. 1984. *Issues in irrigation agriculture and command area development,* New Delhi, Ashis Publications.

Siva Mohan M.V.K.1990. Management process in development with reference to nagarjuna sagar project right canal, Command Area Development, Ph.D. thesis.

Swarup, Relal. *Encyclopedia and Ecology, Environment and Pollution Control.*

Seminar and Workshops

Nag, B.S. and G.N. Kapthalia, Proceedings of the Second World Congress, Vol, Central of Irrigation & Power, *Water Resources of India, in Water and Human need.*

Central Board of Irrigation and Power, 1986.Symposium on enveloping criteria for improve. Planning and Management Of Irrigation System Proceedings for Improve. Planning and Management of Irrigation System: Proceedings (vol.1) – New Delhi.

Chambers, R. Irrigation Management: Ends, Means and Opportunities. Paper presented at Workshop at workshop on Productivity And Equality in Irrigation System in India. Lucknow, Giri Institution Of Development Studies, 12-23 Sepetmber. 1982.

Lenton, R. Management Tools for improving irrigation Performance. Paper Presented at the Special Course on Water Management in Irrigation systems. New Delhi, Central Water Commission, 1982,.

Official and Consultancy Reports

Ashopa, V.N. and Tripathi, Command Area Development in Mahikandan, CMA Monograph No. 76, Ahmedabad, Center for Management in Agriculture, Indian institution of Management.

Asopa, V.N. and Singhi, P.M. *commands Area Development Programme: Strategies Performance In India.* (Consultancy Report for Govt. of India), Ahemedabad Institute of Management, 1987.

Centre for science and environment, New Delhi, (1987) *Wrash of the Nature*

Chambers, *R. Rapid Appraisal for improving existing Canal Irrigation Systems. Delhi, Ford Foundation, Discussion*

Centre for Economic & Social Development, Hyderabad –1989. Nagarjunasagar Canal extension project- an economic evaluation.

Estimate Committee (Sixth Lok Sabha), Government of India, Development Of Irrigation Facilities (12th Report). New Delhi, Ministry of Agriculture and Irrigation (Dept of Irrigation) GOI, 1977-78.

For irrigation and agriculture policies, *Vis a vis* and the need for integration see Govt. of Andhra pradesh, *Report of* the Commission for Irrigation Utilization, Hyderabad, Govt of Andhra Pradesh, 1982.

Government of Andhra Pradesh. Committee on Nagarjuna sagar Project tail and areas, Hyderbad, Govt of A.P.

Government of Andhra Pradesh, Note on activities of CADA in 4 minor Irrigation Projects – Ground Water Department-1997.

Jayaraman, T.K. Implementation of warabandi; A management Approach, in K. K. Singh (ED). *Warabandi for irrigated Agriculture in India*. New Delhi, Central Board of Irrigation and Power Publication.

Kamalpuri, U. Nath Performance evaluation Of Irrigation Projects- A case study of Malaprabha Irrigation project: Bangalore, India institute of Management, 1986, Dissertation, Fellowship Programme Management.

Krishna Murthy, C R. 190. Madras Science Foundation. Ganga Action plans In Relation to Ecological Conservation 7 Resource Recovery.

Lenton, R. Management tools For Improving Irrigation Performance, New Delhi. The Ford Foundation, Discussion paper Series

Ministry for Irrigation, GOI. Inaugural address to the conference of state secretaries in charge of command Area Development, New Delhi.

Ministry of Agriculture and Irrigation, Government of India, New Delhi, Sep. 1984 (Mimeo). Report of the Working Group of Command Area Development for Formulation of the plan Proposals for the seventh five-year plan (1978-83).

Ministry of E & F, Government of India, Environmental (Protection) of Pollution Act, 1978.

Ministry of Energy and Irrigation (CAD & WM Division), Government of India, New Delhi, 1982 Report of he High level Committee on organizational Set up of Command Area Development Programme in major and medium irrigation Project and creation of Water Management and land development Wing in State Irrigation Departments.

Ministry of Water Resources, Govt of India, 1995, Evaluation of Command Area Development Programme – Nagarjuna Sagar Project, A.P.

National Commission on Agriculture, Government of India. Most of the National Commission on agriculture-Resource Development New Delhi, Ministry of Agriculture and Irrigation, Government of India, 1976.

National Institute of Hydroecology, Roorkee, 1985-86. Forest Influences on hydrological parameters- status Report.

National Institute of Hydrogeology, Roorkee, sediment Yeld from different Land Uses: Stat Report.

NEERI, Nagpur and Indian Institute of Public Health (IIPH), Calcutta (1990) *Impact Assessment of Ganga Action Plan on Public Health.*

Planning Commission, India. *Seventh & Eighth Five Year plan.*

Ramakrishna, V., Siva Mohan, M.V.K.., et al 1979. Commands Area Development authorities – a study on Organization and Multi beed Consideration, Hyd., ACI, 1979.

World Bank (EVSP) The World Bank participation source Book.

World Bank OED Précis- 1996. World Bank Lending for large dams- a Preliminary review of impacts.

Index

Agarwal 173
Aggarwal and Narain 171
AIIMS 150
Air Pollution 169-72
Air Pollution (Prevention and Control) Act, 1981 (Revised in 1987) 47, 53-56
Allahabad University 28
Alternative to Big Dams 134-35
Arora 172-73
Ashoka 39
Atmosphere and Climate 82-83
Atomic Energy Act (Radiation Protection Rules), 1971 47
Atomic Energy Commission 109

Balu 168
Bankim Chandra 40
Barbara 178
Bhartiya Wild Life Organization, Dehradun 44
Bhumbala 130
Bidi and Cigar Control Act, 1961 47
Biodiversity 68-69
Bio-geographical Classification of India 62-63
Birth and Death Rates and Life Expectations 111-12
Bombay Natural History Society, Mumbai 44
Botanical Survey of India 70
Brittan et al 175
Broadbent 177
Broker 181
Brudland 31

Canal Irrigation and Mechanical Farming 103
Central Arid Zone Research Institute, Jodhpur 88-89
Central Pollution Control Board (CPCB) 54
Central Water Commission 129, 134, 136
Central Water and Power Commission 130
Climate of Thar Desert 87
Cohen et al 178
Conservation of Plant Kingdom 72
Crocodile Breding and Management Project 76-77

Dakshini 173
Damodar Valley Corporation/ Water Pollution Control) Regulating Act, 1948 46
Dams and Forests 133-34
Dave 171
Deodhar and Nath 173
Dixon 166
Dole and Hill 169
D'Souza 176
Dudgeon, P. 28
Dube 176

Earth Summit, 1992 42
Ecological Research and Training Centre, Bangalore 44
Ecology 27-29
Ecology, Branches of 29-30
Endangered Animals 74-75
Endangered and Endemic Species 69-70
Endangered Vegetation 70-71
Endemic Plants 71-72
Energy Resources 106-09
Environment, Components of 9
——, Holocoenotic Concept on 12
——, Impact of Man on 19-20
——, Measures to Protect 20-21
——, in the Present Context 26-27
——, Segments of 10-12
—— and Technology 40-41
——, Types of 9-10
Environment Protection Act, 1986 47
Environment Pollution, Consequences 163-64
Environmental Awareness and Perception 167-69
Environmental Degradation 21-24
Environmental Education Centre, Ahmed Nagar 44
Environmental Ethics 36
Environmental Factors 13-14
Environmental Impact Assessment 40-41
Environmental Pollution 166-67
Environmental Problems and their Types 20
Environmental Science, Scope and Importance of 15
Environmental Studies, Multi-disciplinary Nature of 14

Factory Act (Pollution and Pesticides) 1948 40
FAO 116
Feijoo and Mmo 169
Florey et al 170
Food Resources 99
Forest (Conservation) Act, 1980 (Revised in 1988) 47
Forest Degradation 90-91
Forest Resources 90
Friends of the Earth 44

Gadgil 176
Gajendragad 172
Gandhi 31
Gilpin 159, 166, 170
Gir Lion Project 76
Goude, A. 8
Govind Ballabh Pant Himalayan Environment Organization, Almora 44
Green Peace 44
Green Revolution 100-02
——, Effect of 102-06
Gurunanak Bani 39
Gyabaah, Nsiah 182

Haryana Agricultural University 130
Heller et al 170
Hot Spots 80-81
Housing Environment 175-77
Hronee 171

Hunter 176
Hwash 158
Hwash et al 181

Increasing Waterlogging 131
India as a Mega-diversity Nation 63-68
Indian Board of Wild Life 77
Insecticide Act, 1968 47
International Biological Programme (IBP) 28, 44
International Union for Conservation of Natural Resource 70
Irrigation Facilities 96

Jhamtani 154
Jim Corbett Park 78

Kak 178
Kandapal and Maheshwari 171
Karan 168
Kayastha 173, 178
Kayastha and Yadav 168
Kerlinger 152
Khosoo 167
Kunwar 180
Kumar and Mathur 177

Land Resources 83-87
Linsely and Franzini 138
Literacy 112-13
Lowenthal 167

Mineral Resources 106
Mines and Mineral (Regulation Development) Act, 1947 46
Mishra 176
Mishra and Prasad 176
Mohsin 176
Morchandreas et al 171
Municipality Act, 1959 46
Narayan 168
National Commission on Agriculture 104
National Council of Agricultural Research 115
National Parks and Sanctuaries 77-79
National Population Policy (NPP) 115
Natural Resources 81
Noise Pollution 177-80
Nuclear Power 107

Odum, Eugene P. 28
Oil and Natural Gas Commission 108
"Our Collective Future" 31

Park, C.C. 8
Patel 175
Plantation of Trees to Check Expansion of Desert 88-89
Pollutants, Types of 17-18
Pollution 15-16
Pollution Control, Fundamental Principles of 19
Population, Density of 113
Population Explosion and Urbanization 110-11
Population Growth Rate 112
Population Policy 114
Population Size and Growth Rate 111
Potential Capacity 135-36
Prakasam 174
Prasad et al 174
Prevention of Food and Adulteration Act, 1954 46, 51
Public Awareness 41

Quran 40

Rajasthan Noise Control Act, 1961 47
Ramprasad 176
Rao 154

Rao, Manohar 167
River Board Act, 1956 46
Rural Settlements 114
Salinity of Water 105-06
Sanctuaries 79
Sathanasaijan 166
Sharma 166
Smith 177
Smith et al 172
Social and Cultural Impact 117-20
Social and Environmental Impacts 126-29
Social Issues and the Environment 30-31
Social Problems 35
Socio-cultural Pollution 180-83
Southwick 173
Spengler et al 171
Stone 168
Sustainable Development, Definition of 122-24
Sustainable Water Resource Development 141-46

Tanuja 180
Tata Institute of Fundamental Research 109
Taylor 15
Tewari 172
Thar Project 76
Thar Desert Biosphere Reserve 89
Thar Desert, Division of 86-89
Tirupataiah 156
Tribal Settlement 114
Transley, Sir Arthur 28

UN 41-42, 45
UNEP 141
United Nations Environment Programme 44
Unsustainable to Sustainable Development 31-32
UN World Commission on Development and Environment 42
Upadhyay, Chitrangad 169
Urbanization Trends 113-14

Varalakshmi 180
Verma and Warner 177
Vijayaraghavan 168, 180

Water for Hydroelectric Power 96-97
Waterlogging 104-05
Water Pollution 172-75
Water (Prevention and Control of Pollution) Act, 1974 (Revised in 1988) 47, 54, 56-61
Water Resources 92-93
Water Resources Development and Environmental Effects 138-39
Water Scarcity, Growing 97-99
Watershed Management Programme 99
Water, Utilization of 94-96
WHO 160, 175
Whyte 168
Wild Life (Protection) Act, 1972 (Revised in 2002) 47, 89
Wild Life Conservation 76-77
World Bank 125
World Commission on Environment and Development 169
World Conservation Monitoring Center 44
World Conservation Unit 44
World Wild Life Fund 44